Breanna,

We Believe in You a... ...ong leader.

We Pray a New ...... Identity of Leadership will rise up inside You as You Read, Study + Apply the words in this Book.

Bless You.

Sam + Joees

ISAIAH 61: 1-3

You the Leader is a "must-read" for any person who feels called to leadership in the body of Christ. Dr. Pringle's insight, gained from over thirty years of pastoral ministry, is practical, biblically based, and includes thinking in the area of leadership that I believe to be revolutionary in the contemporary church.

—Joyce Meyer
Joyce Meyer Ministries, St. Louis, Missouri, U.S.A.

Phil Pringle is an apostolic leader "par excellence." He is also one of those few leaders who knows how to mentor others and to communicate what he knows. *You the Leader* is crammed full of extraordinary insights that will help you become the dynamic leader God wants you to be! I highly recommend it.

—C. Peter Wagner
Chancellor, Wagner Leadership Institute, U.S.A.

I would like to recommend *You the Leader* by Dr. Phil Pringle. All true Christians are called to use their talents and gifts in a position of authority in the body of Christ. This book will help each Christian understand his or her role in the body of Christ.

—Dr. David Yonggi Cho
The Yoido Full Gospel Church, Seoul, South Korea

Phil Pringle's outstanding leadership skills have been proven over many years, and so he is well qualified to write this exceptional book on leadership.

—Pastor Brian Houston
General Superintendent, Assemblies of God, Australia
Senior Minister, Hillsong Church, Sydney, Australia

Phil Pringle is a true leader of leaders. He has a fresh, unique way to look at everything, and there is a strong anointing on his life and ministry. He writes from a wealth of knowledge and experience. This book is certainly deserving of our attention.

—*Pastor Rick Shelton*
Senior Minister, Life Christian Center,
St. Louis, Missouri, U.S.A.

Phil Pringle has been at the forefront of radical church leadership for many years. At Christian City Church he has pioneered many different areas of ministry, gleaning valuable insight and wisdom along the way.

—*Pastor Colin Dye*
Senior Minister, Kensington Temple, London, England

Phil Pringle's new book *You the Leader* is a must for all in leadership or aspiring to be a leader. Anything Pastor Phil writes is excellent because he practices what he preaches.

—*Pastor Kevin J. Connor*
Senior Minister, Waverly Christian Fellowship,
Melbourne, Australia

I subsidized the purchase of one copy of *You the Leader* for each of the leaders in my church—this is a book that can be applied to practical leadership in the local church.

—*Pastor Gordon Moore*
Senior Minister, Christian City Church,
Bridgeman Downs, Australia

Inspiring, thought-provoking, challenging. I just had to buy a copy of *You the Leader* for all my leaders.

—*Russell Evans*
Director, Planet Shakers, South Australia, Australia

YOU *The* LEADER

YOU *The* LEADER

PHIL PRINGLE

WHITAKER
HOUSE

YOU THE LEADER

Phil Pringle
Christian City Church Oxford Falls, Australia
website: www.ccc.org.au

ISBN-13: 978-0-88368-814-4
ISBN-10: 0-88368-814-X
Printed in the United States of America
Australia: © 2003 by PaX Ministries Pty Ltd.
United States of America: © 2005 by Phil Pringle

ய
WHITAKER
HOUSE
1030 Hunt Valley Circle
New Kensington, PA 15068
www.whitakerhouse.com

Library of Congress Cataloging-in-Publication Data

Pringle, Phil, 1952–
You the leader / Phil Pringle.
p. cm.
Summary: "Practical insights into effective church leadership that can be applied in every arena of life, with an examination of the attributes of dynamic leaders and the kingdom principles that govern their lives"—Provided by publisher.
Includes bibliographical references and index.
ISBN-13: 978-0-88368-814-4 (trade hardcover : alk. paper)
ISBN-10: 0-88368-814-X (trade hardcover : alk. paper)
1. Christian leadership. I. Title.
BV652.1.P719 2005
253—dc22
2004028988

1 2 3 4 5 6 7 8 9 10 11 12 **ய** 14 13 12 11 10 09 08 07 06 05

Acknowledgments

G reat leadership alights on the shoulders, not of those who desire to "lord" it over others, but on those who assume the responsibility of doing whatever is necessary to get the job done. It lights on those who respond quickly to serve, those who want to help others get where they want to go, and those who dream of beating the odds and achieving the dream.

A team of these people surrounds me, the "can-do" crowd, leaders who serve. These men and women have teamed together to accomplish a thousand things none of us could ever have done on our own. We believe together; the future is ours. I wake up surprised every day because of the blessing of these awesome men and women whom I have the privilege of leading. Among this army of awesome people is a small group I especially want to mention:

Chris, my sweet wife and closest friend, is one of the greatest team players on earth. Her gifts of hospitality and encouragement have been indispensable in building our great team and our congregation. Together we have sought to fulfill the incredible dreams of God. There is no way I could do what I do or what our church and our movement do without Chris's complete and uncomplaining support. More than support though, Chris is an integral part of the personality of our church. She has always played a major role in forming the culture and vision of our congregation.

Our close friends Simon and Helen McIntyre have been with us from the beginning, faithful and devoted to the dream. Simon, the secretary to Christian City Church International (C_3i), ensures that our movement remains healthy and growing. Greg and Julie French, who are also close, strong friends, head up the pastoral oversight of our church. These two couples have proven to me that team players are not just about people doing the job, but about faithfulness in friendship as kingdom people.

In completing this project, I have been urged onward by many friends and ministers, such as Pastor Kong Hee in Singapore and Pastor Dean Sweetman in the U.S. Thanks for the encouragement, guys! I pray that I can help leaders in this awesome journey.

One of the key people in my world is my personal assistant, Dianne Payne, whose talents are legendary in our part of the universe. She makes my world go round. Thanks also to Jesse Allan who has taken over the reins of managing PaX ministries and producing our books, taking our ministry in this arena into a whole new level of blessing.

Darren Elliot helped with the printing and production of many of our books in their current format. Jeff Crabtree, director of our School of Creative Arts, helped me immensely with his editing and proofing skills. Thanks also to Simon McIntyre, Kerry Palmer, Steve Wood, and Robyn Stanard for taking time to help with various stages of proofing and comments.

Finally, as this new hardback edition of *You the Leader* goes to press in the U.S., I wish to thank deepercalling media and Whitaker House for the hard work that they have invested in furthering our vision.

—Phil Pringle

Contents

one

LEADERS NEEDED

There was a man sent from God,
whose name was John.
—John 1:6

When Winston Churchill was made War Minister at an age when most would be readying for retirement, he proclaimed to his wife, "I believe I was born for this hour!"

These are the types of leaders we need today, leaders who are passionate about leading and hungry for leadership. Leaders who rise above mediocrity while attaining excellence. Leaders who want to lead and who lead well.

In short, we need more Winston Churchills.

We all know we need leaders. Without leadership, anarchy ensues. But we need more than just leaders. In fact, we even need more than just *good* leaders. We need *great* leaders.

Nobel Peace Prize winner Bishop Desmond Tutu once said, "I am a leader by default only because nature does not allow a vacuum." When Bishop Tutu spoke these words, he succinctly captured the powerful truth that leaders are always in demand. Humankind is wired to provide leadership, but it is also designed to need leadership. As strong as the desire to lead might burn in the hearts of some men and women, the desire to be led burns even stronger in the hearts of all people. Leadership is a must when it comes to humanity.

Humankind is wired to provide leadership, but it is also designed to need leadership.

The tragedy begins when the responsibility for filling this leadership vacuum is left to subpar leaders.

When men and women ill-equipped to provide direction and guidance are the ones we put in charge.

When the leadership vacuum is filled by those least qualified to fill it.

Unfortunately, this is the predominant portrait of our times. As always, there is a high demand for leaders, but the quality and quantity of an able and willing supply is not what it could—or should—be.

In today's climate of uncertainty and change, financial upheavals and shifting morality, people everywhere need strong, godly leaders. Our society has spiraled into a state of relativity, of absolutely asserting that there are no absolutes! Leaders who can provide hope and inspiration, steadiness and stability, moral guidance and direction are in high demand.

These are the kinds of people who should be filling our leadership vacuums.

And this is why you need to be a leader.

WORLD CHANGERS

Did you ever stop to think about the prominent role locusts played in the lives of biblical leaders? Moses, for instance, the leader charged with the task of guiding God's chosen people out of Egypt, was responsible for communicating the Lord's will to the Egyptian ruler, Pharaoh. When Pharaoh refused to obey the Lord's commands, Moses was also responsible for conveying the consequences to Pharaoh—one of which was the land being overrun by locusts: *"If you refuse to let My people go, behold, tomorrow I will bring locusts into your territory"* (Exodus 10:4).

Leaders who provide hope, steadiness, and moral guidance are in high demand.

And remember John the Baptist? The spiritual leader who prepared the way for Jesus' earthly ministry? Locusts played a prominent role in his life, too; they're what he ate every day:

> *And John himself was clothed in camel's hair, with a leather belt around his waist; and his food was locusts and wild honey.* (Matthew 3:4)

****

But a much greater similarity, aside from the locusts, exists between Moses and John. In a nutshell, these men were world changers. Their greatest similarity lies in the fact that they both revolutionized their world.

As world changers, there are several common bonds between Moses and John—common bonds that we'd do well to mirror if we desire to be good leaders ourselves.

BOND #1: LEADERS CHANGE THE WORLD

The first bond is pretty obvious: Leaders change their worlds. For Moses, this meant setting an entire nation of oppressed people free. For John the Baptist, this meant changing the hearts of the men and women around him and preparing them for the coming of the Messiah. Each leader radically changed his world—and all the world as a consequence.

The examples don't end here. Across the span of human history lie a host of outstanding individuals who have led the world through difficult times, changed the way we live, and brought about entirely new living conditions for people everywhere. Consider these individuals:

❖ Alexander the Great, king of Macedonia (356–323 BC), changed the political and social climate of much of the civilized world after conquering it by age 33. Having never lost a battle, he introduced new ideas for governing and spread Grecian culture throughout the world.

❖ Renaissance painter, architect, inventor, and engineer Leonardo da Vinci (1452–1519) changed the world by designing innovative bridges, highways, weapons, costumes, and scientific instruments. He invented prototypes of flying machines, the helicopter, and the parachute, and made hundreds of other discoveries during his lifetime.

❖ Adventurer Christopher Columbus changed the world by sailing across the unknown Atlantic Ocean in 1492, unintentionally opening up the New World to all of Europe.

❖ German reformer Martin Luther changed the world on a spiritual level by nailing 95 theses against the practices of the Catholic Church onto the door of the Wittenberg castle church, thus sparking the Reformation.

❖ Dr. David Livingstone (1813–1873), the Scottish missionary and explorer, changed the world when he opened up the deep heart of Africa in 1849.

❖ Inventor Alexander Graham Bell permanently changed the world's communication mode when he invented the telephone in 1876.

The greatest leader of all time, Jesus Christ, continues to transform millions of lives.

Since great leaders change their worlds, it's no surprise then that the greatest leader of all time, Jesus Christ, transformed—and continues to transform—the lives of millions of people. He has irreversibly changed our world for all time. As God in the flesh, He is unlike any other leader who has ever graced this planet. He has brought eternal salvation to all who will receive Him, and He has changed the eternal destinies of innumerable men, women, and children.

BOND #2: LEADERS IMPART VISION

Leaders also impart vision. In the case of Moses, it was imparting the vision of the Promised Land and the exodus it would take to get there. In the case of John, it was imparting the God-given vision of the Messiah who was to come.

In short, we need leaders because they see things that others don't. When we follow great leaders, their vision becomes ours. We start to see what they see, and we begin to own a vision larger than ourselves.

The importance of vision can't be overlooked. Vision is essential if a leader is going to succeed in his or her goals. As Elizabeth Proust said during her term as Secretary of the Department of Premier and Cabinet for Victoria, Australia, "If you get the vision right, we can get everything else right."

Vision comes first. We need visionaries for leaders because they are creative problem solvers who get things done. These are the men and women who...

❖ Can see a city rising out of a swamp, like Sir Bruce Small, who created Surfers Paradise in Queensland, Australia.

❖ Can see a man walking on the moon when U.S. astronauts have yet to make even a single orbit around the earth, like John F. Kennedy and the NASA team.

❖ Can see a one-mile record being broken when medical science declares it is impossible to run a mile in less than four minutes, like Roger Bannister.

❖ Can see the armies of Nazi Germany being defeated when his forces have just been evacuated from Dunkirk by a motley collection of fishing trawlers and small ships, like Sir Winston Churchill.

❖ Can see whole tribes and nations of people being physically and spiritually filled, like Lester Sumrall, founder of Feed the Hungry.

❖ Can see an opposing giant utterly defeated and lying headless on the ground, like 17-year-old David.

BOND #3: LEADERS CREATE THE NEW AND RECREATE THE OLD

Closely related to the idea of vision is the fact that leaders are creative people. As Philip Selznick said in his book *Leadership and Administration,* "The art of the creative leader is to...fashion an organism that embodies new and enduring values."

Leaders bring their visions to fruition through the creative process.

For Moses, this creative process meant creating a new culture of God-worshippers in the desert. For John, this creative process required creating an environment of readiness for the Messiah.

Leaders are creators. They bring their visions to fruition through the creative process. We see this most clearly in the greatest of all leaders, God Almighty Himself, who saw the earth, the Milky Way, and the entire universe of planets and then brought forth that vision in His awesome work of creation. He continues to create today as well, as He redeems the lives of men and women sold out to Him.

Therefore, if anyone is in Christ, he is a new creation; old things have passed away; behold, all things have become new. (2 Corinthians 5:17)

Leaders mirror this creativity in their own lives by hammering out new ideas until they are realities. Great leaders create and positively use their power to shape the future.

Bond #4: Leaders Mentor and Empower

Leaders are also cultural engineers, what I like to call "value designers." They lead the men and women around them to higher levels, taking these individuals beyond where they would go if left to themselves and on to achieve their maximum potential. They make things happen rather than waiting to see what will happen first.

Leaders are cultural engineers; they lead men and women around them to higher levels.

Great leaders stretch the abilities of those they lead. We don't realize our potential until a coach-style leader takes us where we didn't think we would or could ever go.

In August 1971, when I walked into a Sunday evening service of a church in Christchurch, New Zealand, I heard the Gospel of Jesus Christ clearly presented for the first time in my life. As Dennis Barton preached, I was moved to receive Christ as my Savior. Dennis and his dear wife, Barbara, became powerful influences over my life. They took a deep interest in my wife, Chris, and me and the friends we brought to church. Soon after that time, hundreds of young people began turning to the Lord in that church.

There was a great deal of opposition to this move of God. In fact, just after the pastor and his wife took over leadership of that church, an entire group walked out in protest. However, the Bartons were resolute and held to the call on their lives.

Spiritual orientation directly determines our beliefs, values, attitudes, and motivations.

Today, I am so thankful they did. They paid the price that so often accompanies leadership in the kingdom of God, and we have reaped the benefits. Chris and I began a life that we've never regretted, a life of ministry for the Lord. Dennis and Barbara became role models for our young Christian lives. Through them, we learned how to love people and how to release young men and women into the ministry.

Because they allowed us to get involved in ministering to others and gave us early roles of leadership in the church, we developed more quickly than we would have in any other way. We found ourselves doing things we never thought we would, or could, because of the leadership God had placed over our lives.

Now thanks be to God who always leads us in triumph in Christ.   (2 Corinthians 2:14)

In his book *Power, The Inner Experience,* psychologist David McClelland states,

People are strengthened and uplifted by exposure to a charismatic leader....They feel more powerful rather than less powerful. The leader arouses confidence in his followers. They feel better able to accomplish whatever goals he and they share.

This is exactly the type of leadership the Bartons lived out. They are gifted in drawing out the latent potential in others and helping them grow into their God-given destinies. The church needs more men and women like this to mentor and empower God's children for service.

BOND #5: LEADERS SPIRITUALLY INSPIRE

Spiritual leadership is the most important and powerful kind of leadership. Spiritual leadership is a significant basis of influence because it directly affects our spiritual orientation—and consequently, the whole of our lives. For it is this orientation, our spiritual orientation, that directly determines our beliefs, values, attitudes, and motivations.

Once again, consider Moses. His primary role was to lead God's children out of Egypt and into the Promised Land. During this time, he served as an important spiritual leader, simultaneously communicating God's law and love to the people as he led them through the desert.

John the Baptist, too, was as spiritual leader. His primary purpose was to prepare the way for the Lord.

There was a man sent from God, whose name was John. This man came for a witness, to bear witness of the Light, that all through him might believe. He was not that Light, but was sent to bear witness of that Light. (John 1:6–8)

An overview of Israel's history reveals the influential power of spiritual leadership. For the most part, the pattern was the same: Under good kings, the nation followed God and rose into prosperity. Under evil kings, the nation turned from God and fell into corruption.

As the old saying goes, "What walks in fathers, runs in children." This was nowhere more true than in Israel, for when the "father" (that is, the king) did evil, the people did evil, too. But when a king did good, the people did good as well. These leaders, like all leaders, served as behavioral models.

God desires leaders who are sold out for Him, for it is these leaders who can change the world.

Their influence, however, extended beyond just morals. How these leaders acted on the outside (their moral behavior) reflected what was happening on the inside (their spiritual health). And since what walks in fathers, runs in children, whatever morals and spiritual health these leaders displayed, their followers typically displayed the same.

We do not need leaders like Rehoboam, the king of Israel who plunged his nation into idolatry. *"He forsook the law of the LORD, and all Israel along with him"* (2 Chronicles 12:1). Instead, we need leaders who, like Moses, hold up Christ and point constantly to the cross: *"Just as Moses lifted up the snake in the desert, so the Son of Man must be lifted up, that everyone who believes in him may have eternal life"* (John 3:14–15 NIV).

God Builds People To Build His Kingdom

Although the secular world most often excludes God from their how-tos of success, books like the widely read *In Search of Excellence* confirm the necessity of good, moral leadership:

> What we found was that associated with almost every excellent company was a strong leader (or two) who seemed to have had a lot to do with making the company excellent in the first place. Many of these companies...seem to have taken on their basic character under the tutelage of a very special person.... It appears that the real role of the Chief Executive Officer is to manage the values of the organization.

God works through leaders, and He desires leaders who are sold out for Him, for it is these leaders who can positively change their world, impart vision, create new and recreate the old, mentor and empower those around them, and spiritually inspire those they lead.

God, the ultimate Leader, entrusts leadership positions to those who have been tested by fire.

Rest assured, becoming a leader is not all sweetness and light. The making of a leader is a mixture of triumph and failure, blessing and pain. It takes much longer than anticipated, costs more than we want, and takes us on a journey through far more trouble than we ever thought we could manage.

But through it all, God, the ultimate Leader, is graciously shaping us along the way. He entrusts leadership positions only to those He has tested and brought through the fire, and trials are simply par for the course.

Many people begin the race but don't finish. Many plateau once they find a level they're comfortable with. But true leaders are always pressing on further into the purposes of God.

Are you ready to press on into God's purposes?

Are you ready to be the leader?

two

THE LEADER AND HIS GOD

The world changes from the top down, not the bottom up.

Moses stands out in history as one of the clearest examples of the principle that the world changes from the top down, not the bottom up. We already saw in chapter one how Moses delivered three million Hebrews from Egyptian oppression and then formed the great nation of Israel from the raw material of ex-slaves.

This God-appointed and anointed visionary leader took hold of the slaves and their families and led them out—out from under the thumb of Pharaoh. Without his leadership, it wouldn't have happened. It took one man, leading from the top down—as he himself received orders from the ultimate Leader—to get it done.

Moses, Man of God

God molded Moses for this crucial role over a period of eighty years: forty years as a prince in the courts of Egypt's pharaoh and then forty more in the desert as a shepherd tending sheep for his father-in-law.

After leading the Hebrews out of slavery, Moses ascended Mount Sinai in the desert to meet with God. He spent six weeks at the summit, fasting and basking in the presence of God.

Our personal relationship with God must occupy first place in our lives.

Unfortunately, in the absence of their leader, the new nation fell away from God, returning to the debauchery of Egyptian idol worship. They appointed Aaron as their leader, who promptly did what they told him to do: make a golden calf for them to worship.

Nothing angered God more than credit for what He had done being given to another, to a false idol, to a nothing. Aaron was not a leader—a spokesman, perhaps, but not a leader—because he was more a puppet of the people. Orders came from the bottom up, and in this case, the results were disastrous.

When Moses returned, descending from the heights, he was aghast. The people had fallen away from Yahweh so quickly. He smashed the holy tablets marked with the finger of God Himself. The people did not deserve such special gifts. He called on the rabble to make their choice: Those who were for Yahweh were to gather around and stand with him, and those who were not were to stay where they were. Once the difference was clear, he called on the God-fearers to slay those who opposed them, regardless of family ties or friendships. (See Exodus 32:25–28.)

LEADERSHIP LESSONS FROM MOSES

Our personal relationship with God must occupy first place in our lives just as it did in the life of Moses; earthly relationships take second place. Moses established this principle clearly in his life. His ordering the slaughter of the unfaithful was a ruthless act, born out of righteous jealousy for the holiness of God. Certainly it was not designed to gain votes, achieve consensus, or win any kind of popularity— except with his God. That relationship always came first.

The kingdom leader must have the strength of God in his or her soul.

Just as Moses was a man of God, the kingdom leader needs to be a man or woman of God. The kingdom leader must have the strength of God in his or her soul. The example of Moses also shows us that, in the absence of a godly leader, weak, corrupt leaders arise and lure people away from God. The presence or absence of leadership is not all that matters; the quality of leadership is crucial, too.

The absence of strong, upright leadership creates anarchy. As we discussed in the last chapter, nature abhors a vacuum, and anarchy is just a vacuum of moral governing leadership, which attracts bad leaders to fill the void.

Bad leaders destroy nations. Bad leaders draw people away from God. Bad leaders take people backward. In the kingdom of God, bad leaders wreck churches, wound the work of God, and deliver reproach to His people. We must engage in developing leaders who draw believers and unbelievers to God, not away from Him. Our task is not just about the raising up of leaders, but the raising up of godly leaders, leaders with integrity and strength of character. The pressing need in our generation is to develop great leaders for the future.

The soaring need in our generation is to raise up great leaders for the future.

It's tempting to think that God can only use us if we're different, more like one of those heroes of the past. We enshrine such heroes as David, Moses, Daniel, and Abraham, setting them apart in our imaginations as superior beings who are far more qualified than the rest of us "mere mortals."

However, the Bible has always been ruthlessly honest about its heroes. Their successes and their failings are faithfully recorded without veneer, helping us to know we all breathe the same air, are all made of the same flesh, and are basically no different from one another.

For example, *"Elijah was a man with a nature like ours ["a man subject to like passions as we are"* (KJV)]" (James 5:17), yet with all of his imperfection and fallibility as a human being, God changed the course of the weather for three and a half years in answer to his earnest prayers. No matter who we are or how weak and flawed we perceive ourselves to be, we have the opportunity to be used by God and to be successful leaders.

SUCCESSFUL LEADERS WORK FROM WHO THEY ARE

Successful leaders are not artificial clones or plastic imitations of others. They have discovered who they are. They know what they want and where they want to go. They also know what they don't like, what they don't want, and where they don't want to go.

Successful leaders enjoy being who they are. They enjoy their tastes, their clothes, their friends, and their style. Whatever they don't like, they work to change. They are comfortable with who they are. And if there is something they can't change, they change their attitude toward it, seeing it in a constructive light and as a positive attribute.

Once we learn to celebrate our lives instead of rejecting ourselves, we can love others can more fully and more easily accept their differences, which are complementary to us. Rather than diminishing us, they expand our horizons. God includes a diversity of personalities as part of His recipe in the total team vision for success in the kingdom.

THE SUCCESSFUL LEADER IS A GOD-SEEKER

Leaders don't find their foundations for influence in themselves, but in God. Without God they forfeit their destiny and the destinies of those who follow them. David, the ancient and great king of Israel, knew the secret. He loved God. He wanted God, so he sought Him:

> *O God, Thou art my God; I shall seek Thee earnestly; my soul thirsts for Thee, my flesh yearns for Thee, in a dry and weary land where there is no water.*
>
> (Psalm 63:1 NASB)

There are numerous examples of this principle in action throughout history. For instance,

❖ John Knox, the famous Scottish revivalist preacher, is and was famous for his power in prayer. Queen Mary ("Bloody Mary") said she feared his prayers more than Europe's armies. [5]

❖ The English relied on God's providence under the leadership of Queen Elizabeth I in 1588, while the Spaniards relied on power. When the Spanish Armada attacked the British fleet, Elizabeth, the warrior queen, committed her life and the nation to God as she spoke to her troops and inspected her soldiers before battle. As a result, a storm arose and destroyed 65 of the armada's 130 ships; the English lost not a single ship. After this victory, the English government struck a victory medal with this inscription: "God blew and they were scattered." [6]

E. M. Bounds touched on a powerful truth when he wrote the following:

> The preacher must primarily be a man of prayer. In the school of prayer, only the heart can learn to preach. No [intellectual] learning can make up for the failure to pray. No earnestness, no diligence, no study, no gifts will supply its lack. Talking to men for God is a great thing, but talking to God for men is greater still. [7]

Similarly, in his book, *I Believe in Church Growth*, Eddie Gibbs noted, "As one studies the histories of growing churches there is one recurring factor—they are all praying churches." [8]

Seeking God and His will ensures His blessing over our enterprises. Seeking God is a principle that knows no partiality for position; it applies to monarchs, pastors, and janitors alike. (See James 2:1–4.) It works for anyone who chooses to be so engaged.

Uzziah, the eleventh king of Judah, ruled for 52 years. He assumed the throne when he was just sixteen years old, after his father, Amaziah, had been slain. Uzziah was the people's choice. He won wars against the Philistines, Arabians, and Meunites; the Ammonites paid him tribute. He strengthened Judah and upgraded life for his people. A great organizer, his fame spread as far as Egypt. (See 2 Chronicles 25:27, 26:1–15.)

Talking to men for God is a great thing, but talking to God for men is greater still.

What was the reason for his greatness as a leader? It's easily found and clearly revealed:

> [Uzziah] *continued to seek God in the days of Zechariah, who had understanding through the vision of God; and as long as he sought the* LORD, *God prospered him.* (2 Chronicles 26:5 NASB)

Asa, whose name means "healer," reigned for 41 years as the third king of Judah. (1 Kings 15:9–24). As he sought after God, he changed the future of Judah, for he started the trend of turning toward God, which was reflected throughout the next five generations of leaders. His immediate successors as leaders of Judah—Jehoshaphat, Joash, Hezekiah, and Josiah—were outstanding in godliness.

Asa also broke generational ties with his own ancestry of idolatrous leaders. His grandmother was Maacah, who was an infamous idolatress and had heavily influenced Judah toward idolatry. Asa began his reign with courageous ruthlessness for God. He deposed this wicked and powerful woman, even though she was his own grandmother. He then destroyed the terrifying image of the idol Asherah she had raised. He also drove out the sodomites and then destroyed all the idols his fathers had worshipped (1 Kings 15:12).

Throughout his reign, as Asa sought God, he enjoyed success and victory (2 Chronicles 14:11). Not only did this great revolutionary leader seek God himself, but he also commanded the entire nation to do likewise. Asa built his leadership on the principle of seeking God because of a prophet's words to him:

> The LORD is with you while you are with Him. If you seek Him, He will be found by you; but if you forsake Him, He will forsake you. (2 Chronicles 15:2)

The same holds true for us today. As long as we seek God, as long as we pray, our leadership will remain intact. As we supply righteous and courageous leadership, we will continue to enjoy victory, achieve our aims, and remain protected.

three

THE LEADER AND HIS VISION

*Leaders actually conceive realities within
themselves before the events have happened.*

God has always achieved His design through individuals. He chooses a person and then works through His choice vessel to accomplish what He desires. E. M. Bounds once stated, "While the church is searching for better methods, God is searching for better men." [9] We see an example of this in the book of Ezekiel, when the Lord was looking for a leader to guide wayward Israel:

> *So I sought for a man among them who would make a wall, and stand in the gap before Me on behalf of the land, that I should not destroy it; but I found no one.*
>
> (Ezekiel 22:30)

No matter what the situation, leadership is key to the health of any group. John Haggai described the need for leadership with this metaphor: "Our world is like an automobile speeding down a highway. Without a driver, it will surely crash. With a driver, it will go where we want it to." [10]

Warren Bennis, as quoted in *In Search of Excellence*, calls the leader a "social architect." [11] When a leader is a God-person, a God-seeker, vision is planted deep inside. God often speaks in pictures to God-seekers, especially to leaders. Pictures are the visual language of the Holy Spirit to reveal God's blueprints for what He wants to build.

We see this truth of visual revelation throughout the Scriptures. Isaiah wrote of the burden of the Lord, which he *"saw"* (Isaiah 13:1). All the prophets are "seers," to whom God reveals Himself through dreams and visions. In the last days, God has promised the impartation of powerful visions to His young people so that they see the awesome possibilities of all that God can do.

> *And it shall come to pass afterward that I will pour out My Spirit on all flesh; your sons and your daughters shall prophesy, your old men shall dream dreams, your young men shall see visions.*　　　(Joel 2:28)

Vision is a combination of faith, goal setting, and stating the mission of the organization.

FAITH AND VISION

The leader is a "can-do" person. He or she is a faith person. He or she is bold, confident, and almost reckless. This is the defining difference between a manager and a leader. Managers simply oversee what's happening, seldom taking action to mold a situation. Leaders, however, believe all things are possible. They laugh at impossibilities and hate negativity. An air of confidence surrounds them. Nothing is too hard or too big. "We can do it," they tell their team, and, remarkably, they achieve amazing results.

Vision is the gift of faith in action. We see this principle lived out in the realm of church leadership quite frequently. C. Peter Wagner concludes that among all the leaders of growing churches that were studied by what is now known as the Fuller Theological Seminary, there is at least one commonality—the gift of faith. He writes,

> A study of the largest churches in America has led to the conviction that the faith of the pastor was one of the main contributing reasons for the church's growth. The spiritual gift of faith was a common denominator found in the pastors of the largest churches. [12]

George Barna has also conducted extensive research on church life in the last decade. He states, "My work with churches has led me to the conclusion that the single most important element in having an effective and life-changing ministry is to capture God's vision for your ministry." [13]

Leaders believe all things are possible. Nothing is too hard or too big.

No matter what the realm of leadership—the home, the workplace, the church, or the community—vision is crucial. Leaders must funnel their faith into action so that life-changing vision results.

Leadership is clear vision. Without eyes, or without light to aid those eyes, we grope in the dark, unsure of our steps, cautious, afraid, and moving slowly. This is not a leader. A leader is bold and can see the future. "Seeing clearly" is imperative for the leader.

Faith is what God works through to effect the visions He has given us. He speaks to us, and then, with the faith we have, we believe what He says. Faith is the conception of what is possible before it is seen: *"Now faith is the substance of things hoped for, the evidence of things not seen"* (Hebrews 11:1). By faith we believe in the impossible becoming possible.

This is what leadership is all about. Leaders see what no one else does. In Ephesians 3:20 NASB—*"Now to Him who is able to do exceeding abundantly beyond all that we ask or think..."*—the Greek word for *"think"* is *noieo*, which means "to exercise the mind or intellect in comprehending, heeding, considering, pondering, perceiving, thinking, understanding, observing, seeing, conceiving."[14] Leaders actually conceive a reality within themselves before the event even happens. This is what a vision really is. It is not just a hope, a wish, or a desire. It is a knowledge that a certain thing is going to take place because of a number of factors:

- ❖ God has spoken a strategy that works.

- ❖ The strategy has been adopted.

- ❖ Realistic plans have been made.

- ❖ The team can see it happening.

When we meditate in the manner described in Scripture, we take our minds into the realm of conception and the place of perception of the purposes of God. Great

THE LEADER AND HIS VISION

leaders of the Bible, such as Joshua and David, thought deeply and continuously about subjects that were invisible to them until they became realities perceived by their spirits. We read in Joshua 1:8 and throughout the Psalms that they meditated on the Word of God until it became a reality within them, not just a theology. They meditated upon visions of the future until they knew that what they were seeing was more than just imagination.

This same conceiving process is what God employs in church growth. We supernaturally see our churches growing; we sense the growth within our spirits. Growth is a reality we experience before we actually have it.

Growth is a reality we experience before we actually have it.

Good leaders hold positive views of the future. We believe God fulfills our dreams, and our dreams are enlarged. Our desires exceed what we currently have and where we currently are.

We ask God to hear our prayers. As we read, meditate, study, and speak the incredible promises of God (2 Peter 1:4), our faith grows. God speaks to us at our level of faith (Acts 14:9–10), and we find ourselves believing what He has said (Romans 10:17). His truth becomes a reality within us until we can see it (Hebrews 11:1). Our organization *is* larger. It has grown. We speak it because it is real. We are not pretending. We know something that did not come to our consciousness by way of the natural senses. Another faculty has released this knowledge: our

∗∗

spirit. It is God's Word in our spirit. It creates a reality that registers in our spirit. We live by this spiritual knowledge and walk in its light.

Faith exists because of reasonable grounds; it is not based on nothing or on wishful thinking. We believe because certain things have happened in the past. Faith comes from the Word of God. We have faith because we seek God and He speaks to us!

> *And without faith it is impossible to please God, because anyone who comes to him must believe that he exists and that he rewards those who earnestly seek him.* (Hebrews 11:6 NIV)

∗∗

We have faith because we live by the laws of the kingdom.

∗∗∗

It is when we seek the Lord that He speaks to us. Consider Habakkuk, who ascended his watchtower and stationed himself on the ramparts to *"see"* what the Lord would *"say"* to him in a *"vision"* that was to be fulfilled in the future (Habakkuk 2:1–3).

Faith is integrally linked with action. *"As the body without the spirit is dead, so faith without deeds is dead"* (James 2:26 NIV). We have faith because we have labored to achieve the results we have seen in our spirits. It is reasonable for us to believe that God will bless our efforts.

When we are generous in attitude and action, "seed faith" is produced. Once a seed is planted, we have faith it will resurface from the ground as a plant. The very act of giving is the same: Giving releases faith that you will receive in return, just as you have planted.

> *Give, and it will be given to you. A good measure, pressed down, shaken together and running over, will be poured into your lap. For with the measure you use, it will be measured to you.* (Luke 6:38 NIV)

We place God first in our choices, first in our priorities, and He is the first we acknowledge in any plan or result.

As leaders, we place God first in our choices, first in our priorities, and He is the first we acknowledge in any plan or result. We seek His counsel as we make plans, seek His provision as we plan resources, and give thanks and glory to Him when the results come through. In fact, we give the firstfruits of the results to God Himself. This places us in a premium position for blessing, and our spirits know it. Confidence rests on these actions.

> *But seek first His kingdom and His righteousness; and all these things shall be added to you.* (Matthew 6:33 NASB)

We have a general attitude of confidence, and we are encouraged because we continually remind ourselves of God's promises to us. We surround ourselves with people of faith. We do not connect with negative people who discourage our faith.

Confidence is the climate in which God moves. Wishing and hoping that an organization will grow won't make it happen. Knowing it will grow and having that attitude is what makes it happen.

Faith begins with a desire, a passion. Dr. David Yonggi Cho says, "You have to have a burning desire in your heart. If you do not have a burning desire, then wait and ask God to impart His desire to your heart. God does not like the lukewarm, for He specializes only in the red hot; if you have that red hot burning desire, then you are going to have results." [15]

Goal Setting and Vision

Goal setting is another integral part of achieving any dream. It is what takes a supernatural vision into the material realm where we can see it being accomplished. C. Peter Wagner has stated,

> For reasons I do not fully understand, some power is released through setting positive goals that otherwise remains dormant. But although I cannot explain it as well as I wish I could, it is a biblical principle that God seems to honor. Goal setting is the modern biblical equivalent to faith, without which it is impossible to please Him (Heb. 11:6). Faith is the substance of things hoped for. Things hoped for are, of course, future. Putting substance on the future is what happens in a faith projection (goal-setting) exercise. [16]

Dr. David Yonggi Cho, who pastors the world's largest church, says of his church's remarkable growth, "The number one requirement for having real church growth—unlimited church growth—is to set goals." [17]

All too often in the Christian community, however, setting goals and objectives has been seen as somehow unspiritual.

Jim Montgomery, the visionary behind the DAWN (Discipling A Whole Nation) strategy, gives an outstanding example of the impact energetic goal setting can have. He tells of the Christian and Missionary Alliance church in the Philippines, where goal setting had tremendous results.

The movement had already grown, in just 75 years, from one church to five hundred churches—with a total of 25,000 members. The group then set a five-year goal to add 400 churches and 40,000 members. In order to reach these goals,

> They set up new committees and training programs. They established hundreds of prayer cells. They set fund-raising goals and developed programs to reach them. They began publishing a monthly newspaper that kept all the churches challenged and informed of their progress. They established a Census of Statistics and charged it with gathering, interpreting, and reporting statistical data. They commissioned each local church to establish its own goals as well as committees for coordinating seminars, prayer groups, and fund raising.

Montgomery goes on to point out setting these goals was precisely what allowed the church to grow.

> The cumulative effect of all this—and much more—was the development of a climate for growth in every facet of CMA work in the Philippines. The normal resistance to change had been overcome....Without their very challenging goals, these changes so essential for increased evangelism and church planting would never have been made. But with the goals and the changes the goals forced them to make, in just five years about

32,500 more people were brought to Christ and into new local churches than would have been at their old rate of growth. Furthermore, with the success of the program, they have continued to set new and ever more challenging goals.

Montgomery also makes the important point that our motives must be proper in setting our goals. Goal setting motivated by selfishness surely is quite different from selfless God-glorifying goal setting.

The Lord surely will not bless those who set goals for reasons of pride, competition, or political benefit. But it does seem that goal setting is a biblical concept that does release tremendous energy and power for great advances in making disciples and planting churches. [18]

Goals must be realistic and achievable. Most of all, they must be believed and be believable. Without faith that we can do it, no goal will ever be achieved.

Remember,

> Those who have the gift of faith
> are growth-oriented, goal-oriented,
> optimistic, and confident. [19]
> —C. Peter Wagner

VISION AND MISSION STATEMENTS

It's bewildering to me that some organizations—even churches—hire consultants to provide them with their mission statement. The consultant looks over the organization, diagnoses its various elements—culture, purpose, products—and then describes what the vision, mission, and direction of that group should be.

Great leaders have vision burning inside them, and nobody else can hold that flame for them. It is the fire in their bellies, their passion.

Vision could be just as well described as "vibration." The leader feels the vision as a vibration. He or she then imparts the feeling to others, who accept the vision and run with their leader to make it happen. The leader has seen something that ignites fire in their souls.

A vision is something worth living for, and it is something worth dying for. In fact, if it is not worth dying for, it is not worth living for. Brave, godly martyrs throughout history have proven time and again that what we as Christians live for is worth dying for.

We've all been to a hotel, restaurant, or shop where the "mission statement" on the wall behind the counter is nothing more than just that—a piece of paper on the wall behind the counter. Many organizations caught the idea of mission in the eighties and believed that if they just wrote it down and posted it in a strategic spot, some kind of magic would weave itself over their efforts. Suddenly, mysteriously, everyone would raise the standard because a document had been prepared and posted.

Vision could be just as well described as "vibration," a vibration the entire organization can feel.

Sure, a mission statement is a good thing, but it has limitations. A mission statement is a reflector, not a creator. A mission statement encapsulates the goals and purpose of a group, but it cannot communicate the energy behind the words. A piece of paper cannot impart the spirit of the vision; only a leader can do that.

The leader feels the pulse of a burning passion and communicates that heat at every opportunity. He or she lives the dream, breathes the vision, sleeps the mission, and eats the goals every day. The leader shares those goals all the time with everyone. It is a vibration the entire organization can feel.

When you have to set down the rules all the time, you know people have not caught the dream. People who have caught the vision instinctively know what is appropriate and what is required. They don't care what it takes; they live to make the dream reality. At the risk of sounding unrealistically romantic, I have to say that unless the hearts of the team members beat with the pulse of the leader's dream, it's never going to fly.

The leader lives the dream, breathes the vision, sleeps the mission, and eats the goals every day.

If the leader is not inspired about what the organization is doing, nobody else will be. Leaders are always meditating on the end result, pacing their emotions through the experience. They can see themselves there at the end result. The organization is growing, and new buildings are being built. The bank accounts are full and overflowing. If it's a church, new churches are starting, the Bible schools are packed, and families are being restored. If it's a business, satellite offices are going up like crazy, business is booming, and sales are like never before. The place is buzzing.

If the leader has this kind of vision, a piece of paper is a paltry substitute for what the vision really is. The glint in this leader's eye communicates to all the employees and volunteers a determination to be the best, to make it to the top, to break through every obstacle.

A piece of paper is a paltry substitute for what vision really is.

The leader is the bell ringer, the trumpet blower, the drum beater, the vibration maker, and the vision caster. He or she gathers people to a distinct purpose. A great leader imparts the burden, inspires commitment, and sets the pace for achievement of God's purpose.

Articulating the vision is a vital part of a leader's responsibilities. In my own life, once I am clear on a vision, I write it down—again and again. I write out our dreams and visions all the time.

My wife, Chris, and I regularly visited a little café on the banks of the river Avon in Christchurch, New Zealand, in the mid '70s. We were pastoring a church in a suburb of Christchurch at the time, but we had a call to birth another church in Australia. We would sit in that café, sipping coffee and drawing on the table napkins what the church in Sydney would look like. The dream needed to be on paper. When we finally opened our church building in Sydney, twenty years had passed from those days in the café. Our new building looked almost identical to the one we had sketched on the napkin all those years ago. I tell people to start dreaming early because dreams take time to come true.

I draw pictures, write documents, and stare off into space as I envision the circumstances I believe God is calling us to. Every time, it all unfolds before our eyes as we simply keep going. Writing it down focuses my mind, our staff, and our whole church toward the great call God has for us. At the beginning of every year, I post our vision and goals for the coming year on screens at the front of the church. We all get to see where we're going. Power is released when we state vision clearly so that people know exactly where we are headed and what we are attempting to achieve.

As I post these goals, I observe two maxims:

(1) Underproject and overperform.

(2) Out of reach, but not out of sight.

Some enthusiastic people want me to post extremely high goals, when in reality these are just hype. I'd rather post a more conservative, attainable goal and then do better than we expected. This approach increases a leader's credibility. If every week the leader receives new inspiration and announces some great project but nothing ever comes to pass, the congregation soon dismisses these ravings with eyeball-rolling unbelief.

On the other hand, if I post goals that I know stretch everyone a little, but can still be accomplished, then we have a great chance of exceeding them. When we announce to the people that although we went for 100 but we actually achieved 200, the whole church cannot help but be encouraged. The faith of our people is enlarged because what we say we will do, we can do—and, in actuality, exceed!

The credibility of the leader is his or her greatest asset. If credibility is undermined, then the power of leadership is also. We cannot have people following us out of sympathy or "supporting" us because they feel we are weak. People should feel inspired, encouraged, and secure in our leadership. They must feel they can trust their leader. They must know that what their leader has said will actually happen!

FOCUSING ON THE VISION

The lion tamer at the circus takes three pieces of equipment into the ring with him—a whip, a small handgun, and a three-legged stool. A stool! Why the stool? The reason is that as the tamer holds the three legs toward the lion, the beast is transfixed and becomes calm. The difficulty of focusing on three legs at once suspends the single-mindedness of the lion. He is confused and undecided.

Indecision and paralysis of action come from a distraction of focus. Attempting too many major goals simultaneously will generally lead to failure. Distraction keeps us from optimum performance.

Just because we can do a number of things doesn't mean we should attempt to do them all.

Jack Nicklaus, known as the "Golden Bear"—the professional golfer whose twenty championship titles set the record for the most major golf tournament victories in a career—began playing golf at the age of ten and won his first major tournament, the Ohio Open, at the age of sixteen. Between 1959 and 1961, when he turned professional, Nicklaus won all but one of the thirty amateur matches he entered. Nicklaus won his first professional tournament at the 1962 United States Open. During his professional career, he also won six Masters tournaments, five PGA championships, three more U.S. Open titles, and three British Open titles. He won the United States Senior Open in 1991 and 1993. [20]

Regarding focus, this very successful man made this memorable statement:

Do one thing, and do it very well.
—Jack Nicklaus

This contrasts the curse that often accompanies multi-talented individuals. The untapped potential in many of these people is prodigious. We all know the unemployed person with more degrees than a thermometer or the singer/songwriter/musician who is still without direction at midlife. Just because we can do a number of things well doesn't mean we should attempt to do them all.

The untapped potential in many people is prodigious.

A welding torch has a wide, weak flame until the welder tightens the nozzle and focuses the fire into a fine point. Only then can the welder melt and fuse metal.

Our lives are much the same. There will always be one main calling on each of our lives. God equips us with gifts for that calling, so we should focus on that one thing. It is necessary to sacrifice everything else to fulfill that call, to focus all our resources on that one goal. Only then will we succeed, for our highest effectiveness comes as we focus our lives on that singular high calling of God!

four

****

THE LEADER IS A WINNER

****

The leader becomes a winner, privately and publicly, through the principles of the kingdom and not those of this world.

People have a strong tendency to react negatively to dreamers. People with purpose contrast the bleak visionless state of many who spend their lives as onlookers. For instance, the jealous sons of Jacob plotted against their younger brother Joseph because of his grand sense of destiny: *"Then they said to one another, 'Look, this dreamer is coming! Come therefore, let us now kill him and cast him into some pit'"* (Genesis 37:19–20).

The leader learns to handle the worst of circumstances that result from the very dream God has planted inside. The leader becomes a winner, privately and publicly, through the principles of the kingdom and not those of this world.

Conquering Inner Space

A leader is essentially defined by the fact that others are following. If no one is following you, it's doubtful you're a leader. Take a look behind. If you are clearing a path, showing people the way, and they're following, then you're a leader.

A leader needs more than just followers, however. A leader needs to be able to conquer space—inner space. Failure to develop internal self-control leads to collapse; when we gain mastery of our souls and our spirits, however, we overcome the wars within (see Proverbs 16:32 and 25:28) and have the equipment to lead others to the same place.

We cannot take people where we ourselves have not been. We won't know the way or how to get there.

The leader faces the same trials everyone else faces, but if the leader fails to master these, he or she holds little chance of ever becoming the person who can lead others into victorious, successful lives. Leaders are out in front, showing the way, taking people to places they have been themselves. Leaders have both cleared the way and walked the path.

The leader understands what it takes to win and how to win. First, he or she overcomes the private wars raging inside and triumphs over internal struggles. The leader knows that this leads to winning on the outside.

A study of three hundred highly successful people—people like Franklin Delano Roosevelt, Helen Keller, Albert Schweitzer, Mahatma Gandhi, and Albert Einstein—reveals that one-quarter of them had serious handicaps such as blindness, deafness, or crippled limbs. Three-quarters had been born in poverty, had come from broken homes, or at least had been raised in excessively tense or disturbed situations. Yet each found what it took to win against the odds, to be an overcomer.

Raise the overcomer in abject poverty, and you have an Abraham Lincoln. Stricken with infantile paralysis, the overcomer becomes a Franklin Delano Roosevelt. Burn him so severely that the doctors say he will never walk again, and you have Glenn Cunningham, who set the world's one-mile record in 1934. Born black in a society filled with racial discrimination? You have a Booker T. Washington, a Marian Anderson, a George Washington Carver, or a Martin Luther King Jr. Label him a "slow learner" or "retarded" and write him off as ineducable, and the overcomer is Albert Einstein.

Leaders need more than just followers. They need to be able to conquer space—inner space.

Leaders know what to think when the pressure intensifies. Quick fixes and cheap thrills are not our hiding place. We go to God in the fire, not away from Him. He is our refuge and our hiding place, not the world.

WORKING FROM THE INSIDE OUT

Leading people into victory is impossible if we haven't gained personal victory in the first place. Once we have victory, we're able to communicate the steps to that place in simple terms—terms that everyone following is able to understand and implement.

More than just talking about victory or success, people who have beaten some adversary have victory in their spirits and impart that very feeling of victory, that same spiritual life, to those they lead.

People who have beaten some adversary have victory in their spirits.

Check out David. He defeated the giant Goliath. Those who were close to him, those he discipled by example, became giant slayers, too. (See 1 Chronicles 20:4–7; 2 Samuel 21:16–17.) The nature of a giant slayer got inside of them. They received an impartation by just being around David. His victory became theirs.

Think about the implications of this for our own lives. As followers of Jesus, we have the opportunity to be around the greatest Victor all the time. Christ slew more than just a giant; He conquered death! We become *"more than conquerors"* (Romans 8:37) by just being with Him. In turn, we can pass on that conquering spirit to those around us.

The Necessity of Trials

Scripture tells us that trials are not strange events for us as Christians: *"Many are the afflictions of the righteous, but the Lord delivers him out of them all"* (Psalm 34:19). If we are going to be conquering leaders, it goes without saying that there will first have to be trials that need to be conquered.

If we are surprised when there is pressure on our lives, then we are badly prepared for the Christian life. If we have swallowed a gospel promising Disneyland Christianity, we'll be severely disappointed.

Trials are inevitable. The further we go and the more responsibility we assume, the greater these trials will become: *"Beloved, do not think it strange concerning the fiery trial which is to try you, as though some strange thing happened to you"* (1 Peter 4:12). It is foolish to ignore the fact that we will encounter pain at times in our Christian walk, especially as leaders. Accepting this fact arms us for the battles we will surely have to face.

> *Therefore, since Christ suffered for us in the flesh, arm yourselves also with the same mind, for he who has suffered in the flesh has ceased from sin.*   (1 Peter 4:1)

THE VARIETY OF TRIALS

Not only are there many trials, but there is also a variety of trials: *"Count it all joy when you fall into various trials"* (James 1:2). In facing these trials, we must first identify the type of trial we are facing and then respond to it correctly. For instance, if it is the Devil, then we must resist, rebuke, and renounce that dark Enemy of our soul (James 4:7). If it is the Lord, however, then we must surrender and worship Him (James 5:13).

In the next chapter, we'll look at some specific leadership challenges as well as how to handle them. There are many trials, and there are many kinds of trials, but with preparation we can be victorious.

five

THE LEADER'S TRIALS

The trials that developing leaders must face are numerous. From life storms and wrestling with God to satanic attacks and ongoing temptations, leaders face a host of challenges that are crucial to their development.

CRUCIAL CHALLENGES TO THE MAKING OF A LEADER

STORMS OF LIFE

As Christians, we build our lives upon the Rock because when storms come—not *if*, but *when*—we will be able to stand.

> *He is like a man building a house, who dug deep and laid the foundation on the rock. And when the flood*

arose, the stream beat vehemently against that house, and could not shake it, for it was founded on the rock.
(Luke 6:48)

Storms are inevitable in life. God is not out to get you, causing every little bump in your life. The Bible reveals that even *"chance"* can be the cause of some things in our lives.

*The race is not to the swift, nor the battle to the strong, nor bread to the wise, nor riches to men of understanding, nor favor to men of skill; but time and **chance** happen to them all.*
(Ecclesiastes 9:11, emphasis added)

In other words, life happens. Things simply come to pass in the normal course of events. We don't have to read deep meaning into every little thing that takes place. We're in danger of becoming neurotic or paranoid if we imagine God is controlling every tiny detail of our lives. It is neither biblical nor sensible to live with this perspective.

God is not so secretive that we're on some everlasting treasure hunt, trying to find His well-hidden plan.

Having said this, there are obviously definite events that the Lord does arrange. These divine "coincidences" are easily recognizable as coming from above. God is not a poor communicator, nor is He so secretive that we are constantly on some everlasting treasure hunt, trying to find His well-hidden plan.

When we do face these "chance" storms of life, the mark of a good leader is a healthy, God-focused response. In Christ, we possess the power for successful responses to every storm: *"For whatever is born of God overcomes the world; and this is the victory that has overcome the world—our faith"* (1 John 5:4 NASB).

A successful response is a rejoicing response. Consider the prophet Habakkuk, who resolved he would rejoice no matter what happened. In other words, he made the choice to rejoice:

> *Though the fig tree may not blossom, nor fruit be on the vines; though the labor of the olive may fail, and the fields yield no food; though the flock may be cut off from the fold, and there be no herd in the stalls; yet I will rejoice in the LORD, I will joy in the God of my salvation.* (Habakkuk 3:17–18)

This is conquering inner space. When disappointments are enormous, when the blows are relentless, when all expectations are dashed—this is when we make the choice, *"Yet I will rejoice in the LORD."*

Private winners overcome powerful negative emotions by bringing them into conformity with the Word.

This person is a private winner. He or she smiles deeply on the inside. This person looks at the trial, smiles, and says, "This will be good for me!" Private winners overcome powerful negative emotions by bringing them into conformity with the Word, no matter how sorry they may be feeling for themselves or how much they would love someone else to.

The weather brings changes to our environment on a regular basis. One day it's rainy, the next day it's clear. The same is true in our circumstances. They are constantly changing, and we have no control over which way the wind blows.

However, we are able to hoist our sails and set them so that we sail forward, upwind! Instead of complaining about the weather, we can take advantage of it. Instead of speaking about the storm, we speak to it! We take dominion in our world. Even though we have no control over external space, we do control our inner space.

> ## Instead of complaining about the weather, we can take advantage of it.

Like Habakkuk, let's choose to rejoice, no matter what blows our way.

CHASTENING

Chastening is another challenge we must face as we develop into good leaders. It comes when we do wrong against God, our Father in heaven.

Plain and simple, there are penalties for wrongdoing. Modern secular thinking, however, seriously fouls up this simple equation. It's popular to think that people who have done wrong are just sick, not sinful; in need of healing, not punishment.

When people do wrong, they are often discouraged from feeling sorrowful or guilty. Instead, they rationalize that their sinful behavior is the result of victimization and mistreatment by others. This thinking negates real justice. Failed justice raises despair to its highest levels, and the value of life plunges as cynicism soars.

Now, God has not changed, and neither has He subscribed to this sort thinking. If we offend God, we will suffer until we get it right. Pain gets our attention more than anything else. Once we've dealt with the issue, His mercy flows in abundance, but mercy will have no meaning if we fail to see that God holds high and holy standards for our lives.

So, what is the purpose of chastening? Through it, we come to understand right and wrong, good and evil. Chastening teaches us to fear the Lord and to respect Him.

I've often heard sincere Christians bravely declare the need for the *"fear of the LORD"* to return to the church. This is not something we just one day decide to own. It is a genuine fear that's learned through experience. I have no qualms in saying I'm terrified of God. I've crossed Him once or twice. He is very big!

We also learn obedience and come to understand justice through the process of chastening. Even Jesus *"learned"* obedience during His time on earth: *"Though He was a Son, yet He learned obedience by the things which He suffered"* (Hebrews 5:8).

As we are chastened, we learn to live inoffensively toward God:

He who has suffered in the flesh has ceased from sin.
(1 Peter 4:1)

Blows that hurt cleanse away evil, as do stripes the inner depths of the heart. (Proverbs 20:30)

Please understand that the purpose of chastening is to bring us closer to the Lord, not to distance us from Him. In fact, even though this may be hard to hear, chastening is actually a signal of His love for us.

And you have forgotten the exhortation which speaks to you as to sons: "My son, do not despise the chastening of the LORD, nor be discouraged when you are rebuked by Him; for whom the LORD loves He chastens, and scourges every son whom He receives."

(Hebrews 12:5–6)

Though my children are now well past the age when discipline involved spanking, I remember the times when the rod was needed. Properly done in love and without anger, spanking actually helps the relationship between parents and their children.

Popular thinking is most often opposed to spanking. In fact, some countries' governments have passed laws making corporal punishment illegal. It is true there have been abuses, but the verbal abuse and emotionally coercive measures parents are forced to employ in the absence of physical discipline can be far more damaging to the minds and hearts of young children. All the threats, quietly menacing talks, yelling, isolation treatment, and other forms of punishment fall way behind the quick, effective administration of a well-controlled rod. Attitudes change almost immediately, since pain teaches the child not to repeat the offense. No child is convinced by mere words.

The purpose of chastening is to bring us closer to the Lord, not to distance us from Him.

I'm not a psychologist; however, I have spent almost three decades pastoring people and leading churches. I've observed that people who have received no chastening in their earlier years struggle a lot more with guilt than those who have. Our inner sense of justice demands satisfaction, no matter what the glossy magazines try to tell us. If we have done wrong, we know it. An unchastened conscience does not rest easily with the internal knowledge of unresolved wrong. Emotions warp under the weight of unresolved guilt within. People who have paid the penalty for their wrongs, though, are free from that weight. They've "paid their dues." Their consciences are clear because justice has been satisfied.

In the same way that punishment from a parent helps a child to grow, God's chastening strengthens our spirits:

> *If you endure chastening, God deals with you as with sons; for what son is there whom a father does not chasten? But if you are without chastening, of which all have become partakers, then you are illegitimate and not sons. Furthermore, we have had human fathers who corrected us, and we paid them respect. Shall we not much more readily be in subjection to the Father of spirits and live? For they indeed for a few days chastened us as seemed best to them, but He for our profit, that we may be partakers of His holiness. Now no chastening seems to be joyful for the present, but painful; nevertheless, afterward it yields the peaceable fruit of righteousness to those who have been trained by it. Therefore strengthen the hands which hang down, and the feeble knees, and make straight paths for your feet, so that what is lame may not be dislocated, but rather be healed.* (Hebrews 12:7–13)

Every person who is born again will be chastened (literally *"scourged"*) by the Lord. It is His kingdom, and we are His family. He goes to work on us so that we will bring Him glory, not shame.

Some of the most terrible times in our lives are those times of chastening from the Lord. Yet afterward, we welcome the changes God has achieved in us. We're easier to live with. Other people enjoy our company because we have a nature much closer to that of Christ. God does, too, and we will even enjoy our own company a whole lot more!

Other people enjoy the company of a person who has the nature of Christ.

Another positive result of discipline is the fruit of wisdom. As the Bible assures us, properly administered discipline results in wisdom:

> *Wisdom is found on the lips of him who has understanding, but a rod is for the back of him who is devoid of understanding.* (Proverbs 10:13)

> *The rod and rebuke give wisdom, but a child left to himself brings shame to his mother.* (Proverbs 29:15)

> *Foolishness is bound up in the heart of a child, but the rod of correction shall drive it far from him.*
> (Proverbs 22:15 KJV)

Through discipline that is based on right and wrong, foolishness departs.

> *By mercy and truth iniquity is purged: and by the fear of the LORD men depart from evil.* (Proverbs 16:6 KJV)

If we desire to reduce the chastening in our lives, we must *"make straight paths for* [our] *feet"* so we can walk a straight line without stumbling. This means establishing a disciplined lifestyle. Walking a straight path brings an end to chastening, and it also brings healing.

Without straight paths, minor ailments become major as lame limbs dislocate (v. 13). And without straight paths, fellowship with good people, as well as with the Lord, is broken. The nourishment that normally flows from fellowship in the body of Christ (see Colossians 2:19) fails to reach the broken limb, and healing becomes impossible. When we are suffering and not wanting to fellowship, this is precisely the time we should strive to surround ourselves with caring, faith-building people.

Further growth also means that we won't live disciplined lives just because we fear the consequences of undisciplined living; rather, we will do so because we desire to please the One we love and because we do not want to offend Him who died for us.

THE DEALINGS OF GOD

The problems we face are not always problems to be solved. Some problems are God's way of changing us. These are the dealings of God transforming us into the image of Christ.

In the beginning it was God's determination to make humankind. This has never changed. God is still making the human race, for He is making us into people who do His will: *"For we are His workmanship, created in Christ Jesus for good works, which God prepared beforehand that we should walk in them"* (Ephesians 2:10).

Some of the arrows used by the Israelites were made from acacia wood, a gnarled shrub that grows in the desert. This strong, knotted wood is hard, heavy, and highly insect repellent. In fact, it is the same wood God used for building the tabernacle in the wilderness (Exodus 36:20).

To make a branch of acacia wood straight, however, was quite an involved task. Before it could be used to make arrows, it had to be soaked in water, pinned to the ground with stakes at the twisted places, and then left to dry in the sun. Oil and water were massaged into it regularly, and eventually a springy, tough arrow or spear was born, capable of flying true to its mark.

God makes us into His men and women in much the same way. Even Jesus was shaped by the hand of God before His release onto the public scene:

> And He has made My mouth like a sharp sword; in the shadow of His hand He has hidden Me, and made Me a polished shaft; in His quiver He has hidden Me.
>
> (Isaiah 49:2)

He transforms us so that He can pour His power into us. He begins processing us the day we give ourselves to Him, as pressures completely unequal to our current level of responsibility build up around us.

On the Potter's Wheel

Another way to think about this transformation process is to consider a potter and his clay. Jeremiah used this illustration in Jeremiah 18:1–11. Now, understand that it is much more difficult for deep changes to take place once we are in leadership. It is far better that these inward workings take place before the day of our release to the public.

How does this process of transformation work?

First, the potter repeatedly forces the shapeless lump of clay through a screen to remove bits of stone, grass, weeds, and air bubbles. The beginning of the call of God is all about removing those things in us that are hindering our growth. These same issues, if not dealt with, will damage our lives in later years, so we must deal with them early on.

God transforms us so that He can pour His power into us.

Sometimes we think we can get away with a few problems, a few air bubbles or blades of grass, and still succeed in the ministry—and we may for a while. However, the damage from this debris will only increase as our load becomes heavier, and we will eventually collapse under its weight.

After the potter removes the clay's impurities, it is then kneaded. The clay becomes softer and more malleable. This is akin to the Holy Spirit softening our hearts to the Lord as He prepares us for molding.

The turning wheel is the next step. The wheel goes round and round. Here is where we learn staying power. We thought we were going to have great adventures, but here we are, going to church—going to work, going to church, going to work, going to church—round and round and round. It is right here—in this repetitive, seemingly boring lifestyle—that God deals with us. We learn to stay where He's placed us.

Then water is poured all over us. "At last!" we think, "This is my great moment! Release to the leadership position He's called me to." No, not yet. The Holy Spirit pours over us like water in such a way that we can be molded further by the hand of God. His thumb presses deep into the center—not on the outside, but on the inside. He goes to work on areas no one else can see. As the thumb of the Potter penetrates the center, we feel the beginnings of being opened up as a vessel for God.

The hands of the Potter get firmer. More water is poured. He squeezes the clay, and it rises. Even while God is squeezing, we grow taller, gaining profile, finding our shape. However, if we have held on to one of those small stones or weeds, here is where it is found out. As the clay walls grow thinner, hidden lumps warp the clay in the Potter's hands. A hard stone cuts right through the wall of the rising pot, and the shape that was forming is ruined. The stone must be found and dug out. We cannot afford any hard attitudes, big or small. We cannot allow this debris to remain in our life.

We cannot afford any hard attitudes, big or small. We cannot allow weeds to remain in our life.

When impurities are revealed, they are removed and then the clay is squashed back into a shapeless lump. The Potter begins again. Once more, water from above is poured out. The firm pressure and squeezing of the Potter begins again. We look a lot more like we should as we stand tall on the wheel. We actually look like a vessel for God!

Then we feel movement. A spatula slides under us. We're on the move. Finally we're going somewhere. We're moving! The potter carries us toward a quiet corner of the room. We say, "No, there's the door, over there." But we're carried toward what could only be described as a shelf. "Oh, no!" we cry. This is not what we want. We want to be out there, doing work.

However, on the shelf we go. We need to calm down and dry out a little. Time passes. It seems like forever. We doubt the call, wondering if God is ever going to use us.

Then, finally, we feel the move of God again in our lives. Yes, yes, yes! We're moving. "The door's over there, Lord."

"We're not going there. We're going over here," He says.

"But this is the hot part of the room. What's it called? The kiln? I've always wondered what this place is. Oh, no! We're not going in there. Not that door—the other one!"

And into the fire we go. We're fired into resilient vessels for God. In the kiln any cracks are discovered immediately. It is here, under intense heat, that God makes His decision to use us or not. We may think we are in charge, but we are not the One choosing whether we will do something for God. It is His kingdom; He chooses His servants. And it is in the fire that this happens: *"I have chosen thee in the furnace of affliction"* (Isaiah 48:10 KJV).

Though this time may seem lonely, we are never alone in the fire. Many years ago, three bound Israelites discovered this when they found Jesus to be present in the fire. It was here that their bonds were broken, and they were set free! (See Daniel 3.) The Lord promises, *"When you walk through the fire, you will not be burned; the flames will not set you ablaze"* (Isaiah 43:2 NIV). The word *"through"* in this passage is very comforting; it indicates that the fire is not forever.

Finally, the firing is over. We're now tough, glazed, and colorful! When we emerge, though, we're not so keen on moving around and getting things done anymore. We've had all personal ambition burned right out of us. Impatience gives way to surrender, and we're actually happy for God to use anyone else. We feel less qualified than ever for service to God. When we come out of the fire, this is just about the time the Lord begins to use us.

He carries us from the room, and we, His vessels, are filled. He fills us with living water for the thirsty, new wine for the despairing, oil of joy for the grieving, and praise for the depressed (Isaiah 61:3). It is then that He commissions us, "Go!"

TEMPTATION

> Here, then, is one of the great and precious truths about temptation. Temptation is not designed to make us fall. Temptation is designed to make us stronger and better men and women. Temptation is not designed to make us sinners. It is designed to make us good. We may fail in the test, but we are not meant to. We are meant to emerge stronger and finer. In one sense temptation is not so much the penalty of being a man; it is the glory of being a man. If metal is to be used in a great engineering project, it is tested at stresses and strains far beyond those which it is ever likely to have to bear. So a man has to be tested before God can use him greatly in his service. [21]   —William Barclay

The first encounter with temptation occurred in the Garden of Eden, where our distant ancestors, Adam and Eve, succumbed to the wiles of Beelzebub (Genesis 3). It was here that sin first entered the world.

Satan's first device in temptation was—and still is—to question the Word of God: *"Has God indeed said, 'You shall not eat of every tree of the garden'?"* (Genesis 3:1). The Word is the final ground of truth. Compromised and diluted, it provides no platform for defense.

Eve's mistake was in answering the Devil. We are told to renounce, rebuke, and resist the Devil, not discuss the matter with him. (See 2 Corinthians 4:2, Jude 1:9; James 4:7.) The most we are ever to do is speak the Word as a sword into the face of the Evil One, but we are not to converse with him, even about Scripture. He is the arch debater, and his talent is deception.

"Temptation is designed to make us stronger and better men and women."

Trust is easily mocked by reason. Eve endeavored to defend God and declared why God had forbidden the fruit from the central tree: *"We may eat the fruit of the trees of the garden; but of the fruit of the tree which is in the midst of the garden, God has said, 'You shall not eat it, nor shall you touch it, lest you die'"* (Genesis 3:2–3). The Devil saw his chance, brazenly denying the Word of God: *"You will not surely die"* (v. 4).

Satan then blasphemed the character of God: "God is holding out on you. He hasn't told you the real reason you shouldn't eat of the tree. *'For God knows that in the day you eat of it your eyes will be opened, and you will be like God, knowing good and evil'"* (v. 5).

Suddenly, Eve had a new view of the tree, a view she hadn't considered before. Focusing on the tree from a new angle, she wondered how there could be any danger in that beautiful fruit. She saw that the fruit was good, that it looked good, and that it could make one wise. *"So...she took of its fruit and ate. She also gave to her husband with her, and he ate"* (v. 6).

God has always desired His people to serve Him because they want to. This can never be without choice. The choice is genuine, heartrending, and tough. Adam and Eve were confronted with the options, and they both chose badly. Innocence suddenly evaporated. A covering (maybe of light) disappeared with their disobedience, and they realized they were naked before God.

Nakedness is embarrassing. They attempted to cover themselves with leaves. Ever since the Fall, our vain efforts to cover our nakedness fall short every time. The only covering pure and permanent enough for eternity is the robe of righteousness (Isaiah 61:10) that Christ freely grants us on the day of our salvation.

Everybody gets tempted: *"No temptation has overtaken you except such as is common to man"* (1 Corinthians 10:13).

Even Jesus? Tempted? Yes! He was tempted in every way you and I are so that He can identify with us: *"For we do not have a High Priest who cannot sympathize with our weaknesses, but was in all points tempted as we are, yet without sin"* (Hebrews 4:15).

The only difference, as this verse shows, is that Jesus remained "without sin." Yes, He was tempted, but He never succumbed.

This was most clearly shown in the second great battle in the difficult terrain of temptation. Here, the Savior of the world and the Adversary of heaven met in the desert of Jeshimon, which lies on the eastern slopes of the Judean Mountains that lead down to the Dead Sea. Jesus was led *"by the Spirit"* (Matthew 4:1) into this wilderness for a battle similar to that fought in Eden.

Understand that the Holy Spirit guided Jesus into this experience. God makes His leader. These processes forge a character of integrity under pressures that the Lord knows we can handle. This time, the pressure was in a desert, not a garden. This time, the pressure was faced alone, not with a companion.

God has always desired His people to serve Him because they want to.

Could this Man—this *"last Adam"* (1 Corinthians 15:45)—be the author of an entirely new race of people? A people for God? The answer to this question could only be discovered on the anvil of temptation.

In preparation for ministry, Jesus fasted forty days and nights. It is an understatement to say that He was hungry by the end of those six weeks (Matthew 4:2). The tempting idea of making a little food for Himself crossed His mind as Satan whispered in His ear, *"If You are the Son of God, command that these stones become bread"* (v. 3).

What could be the problem with that? Surely God in heaven wouldn't begrudge His only Son a little food at the end of a major fast? It certainly seemed reasonable.

However, the real underlying temptation here was not about food; it was about Christ proving that He was the Son of God through an outward miracle and not by inward faith in the Word of God. Jesus discerned this scheme as a dark design from hell, unsheathed the mighty sword of the Spirit, and turned Satan away: *"It is written, 'Man shall not live by bread alone, but by every word that proceeds from the mouth of God'"* (v. 4).

After this came Satan's second temptation of Jesus:

Then the devil took Him up into the holy city, set Him on the pinnacle of the temple, and said to Him, "If You are the Son of God, throw Yourself down. For it is written: 'He shall give His angels charge over you,' and, 'In their hands they shall bear you up, lest you dash your foot against a stone.'"   (Matthew 4:5–6)

Jamieson, Fausset and Brown's Commentary notes that this Scripture would read more correctly as "the Devil conducted" Jesus into Jerusalem, which was the seat of the temple and of all Jewish worship. [22] Herod, in rebuilding and enlarging the temple, had erected a tall gallery overhanging the great ravine of Kedron in the valley of Hinnom. Josephus wrote of being unable to look down and see the bottom from this great height. [23]

And here is where Jesus found Himself being "conducted." Fatigue and hunger from forty days in a wilderness had left Him vulnerable to manipulation. In that unusual suspension of normal thinking, Jesus found Himself staring at an incomprehensible depth from a vast height when the Devil challenged Him to prove who He was by jumping off into this seemingly bottomless pit.

Each of the temptations Jesus faced was designed by the Devil to question His authenticity. As a child, Jesus had progressively grown in the awareness of who He really was. Even though His identity was known from the womb, only a progressive revelation from above had secured that knowledge in His own mind and heart. His development in awareness was the same as everyone else's; His journey needed to have been like ours, and He spent time in the Scriptures and in prayer. However, unlike all other human beings, God spoke into Jesus' spirit that He actually was the Messiah. He added up the circumstances of His birth and of His life, and the equation brought Him to the inescapable conclusion that He was, in fact, the Messiah.

Yet here was Satan, challenging Jesus' authenticity. This area of self-identity and self-doubt is the Achilles heel for almost every one of us. If entertained, self-doubt will keep us from achieving God's purpose every time. This inward sense of destiny demands that we recognize the height of the calling on our lives; at the same time, humility and sanity demand that we neither exalt nor delude ourselves.

For Jesus, as He stood atop the temple, defeating these doubts with a miracle would certainly have helped—even silenced forever—the need to ever prove who He was again. But He discerned the motivation and tone of the question. It was not a question demanding an answer. It was an obvious arrow of doubt aimed at the Word of God and the revelation He had received. He was, and is, the Son of the Most High, Yahweh's firstborn. He didn't need to prove it to Satan under Satan's conditions.

Each of the temptations Jesus faced was designed by the Devil to question His authenticity.

Jesus also understood that action motivated from doubts would only reinforce those doubts. Sometimes, to act in faith is to do nothing. This certainly was the case at this point. Faith was shown by resting in the revealed Word and by seeking no external signs for proof of His identity.

75

Finally, the Devil, feeling the dreadful impact of the Word in the last clash, attempted to employ Scripture himself. He quoted the psalmist—*"For He shall give His angels charge over you, to keep you in all your ways. In their hands they shall bear you up, lest you dash your foot against a stone"* (Psalm 91:11–12)—declaring that Jesus would be protected from harm because God had promised so. The Devil conveniently omitted the following verse—*"You shall tread upon the lion and the cobra, the young lion and the serpent you shall trample underfoot"* (v. 13)—which foretold Satan's own defeat at the hand of the very One he was presently plying.

In this second temptation, Satan tried to ensure the failure or death of Jesus by taunting the Son of God into a duel with death. But Jesus saw through the ploy and rebuked Satan by swinging the great Sword of the Lord: *"It is written again, 'You shall not tempt the LORD your God'"* (Matthew 4:7).

Jesus understood that action motivated from doubts would only reinforce those doubts.

The Devil, more convinced than ever that this Man actually was the Christ, again conducted Jesus to a view of *"all the kingdoms of the world and their glory"* (v. 8). According to Luke, this happened in a *"moment of time"* (Luke 4:5). It was a momentary, supernatural view of the kingdoms of the planet, with the prospect that Jesus could rule them all if He would simply bow down and worship Lucifer.

The Son of God was destined to rule this planet—but not that way. Jesus felt the divine aspirations within, but He was also well aware this was not the path to His glory. The Devil had assumed his most appealing of characters, luring Jesus into entertaining the thought. As the feelings coursed through His emotions and the evil idea trickled into His mind, His spirit was repulsed. With all the might He could muster, He shouted against the Devil, *"Away with you, Satan! For it is written, 'You shall worship the LORD your God, and Him only you shall serve'"* (Matthew 4:10).

The Enemy was scorched under the blistering wrath of God. The impact of the *"rod of His mouth"* (Isaiah 11:4) sent Satan reeling. The Devil fled. This sealed the victory of Jesus over the Adversary—even before the cross. Jesus was ready; His choices had been made, and His faith was intact. Hell trembled.

The purpose of temptation is to strengthen our will. God is not seeking robots that worship and obey Him unwittingly; He seeks people who, when faced with strong compelling options, choose Him.

The best time to choose against temptation is before it is there. We must decide we do not do certain things before we're even faced with them. Then, when we are confronted with the temptation, the choice has already been made. We don't stop to entertain the feelings, and therefore we don't get to the place where we're fighting the lure.

Here is the "why" of temptation: Resisting temptation develops the power of choice. There's little choice in doing evil. As children, doing wrong comes easily to most of us. You don't have to teach a child how to whine, cheat, tell lies, or disobey—those behaviors come naturally, without effort.

But when the pressure from within and without is to do wrong, then to do the right thing takes effort—an exerted effort of the will. Most of us have a lazy will when it comes to doing the right thing. God helps us develop strength inside as we choose to do the right thing. We become stronger, and the right choices become easier.

The best time to choose against temptation is before it is there.

First Corinthians 10:14 tells us to *"flee from idolatry"* so we won't be blocked in escaping from the allure of the Devil. Idolatry loves things more than God. If anything or any person has captured our attention and emotions more than the Lord has, then it needs to be brought down so we are not road-blocked in the escape from temptation.

Our temptations are not unique to us, either. Everyone is tempted. We're all made of the same flesh. None of us face any greater temptations than others do. We may think we do, but we don't. Others have conquered whatever is tempting us; we can, too.

> *No temptation has overtaken you except such as is common to man; but God is faithful, who will not allow you to be tempted beyond what you are able, but with the temptation will also make the way of escape, that you may be able to bear it.* (1 Corinthians 10:13)

We must understand that there is always a way of escape from temptation. God never allows us to be tempted beyond our capacity to overcome. We imagine, at times, that He has—but He hasn't. Whatever we are facing, we are capable of dealing with successfully. The choice is ours. The power is available. The escape route is there.

Overcoming temptation saves us from a horde of difficulties. As John Dryden wrote, "Better shun the bait than struggle in the snare." It is far better to respect the fence at the top of the cliff than to need the ambulance at the bottom.

Self-denial, the essence of Christian living, is an extremely unpopular concept in our age. "Get what you want." "Go where you want." "You deserve it." "Don't sacrifice your life for anyone." "It's your body, so do what you like with it." Every day we face an avalanche of "me-isms," the currently accepted philosophy that ignores basic keys to real life such as sacrifice, self-denial, delayed gratification, and discipline. Yet respect for principled living and the denial of selfish lusts are key to success, inwardly and outwardly.

WARFARE WITH THE DEVIL

Conflict with the demonic realm is inevitable for the Christian, especially for the Christian who's a leader. The obvious premise, *"Strike the Shepherd, and the sheep will be scattered"* (Zechariah 13:7), is something the Devil is attempting to take advantage of constantly. As the purpose of the Adversary is *"to steal, and kill, and destroy"* (John 10:10 NASB), Satan seeks to hinder us any way he can (1 Thessalonians 2:18).

Charles Finney, the noteworthy revivalist of the Second Great Awakening, stated, "Alive Christians often have terrible conflicts. They face temptations that never even occurred to them before: blasphemous thoughts, atheism, suggestions to do evil things, and even to kill themselves. If you are spiritual, expect these conflicts." [24]

Any Christian leader who serves as a leader must grasp victory in dealing with spiritual enemies. Nothing of worth is ever achieved without opposition.

The Devil is the Christian's constant adversary, but we know how to beat the Devil in a fight. Paul declared that *"we do not wrestle against flesh and blood, but against principalities, against powers, against the rulers of the darkness of this age, against spiritual hosts of wickedness in the heavenly places"* (Ephesians 6:12). In short, we wrestle in the spiritual realm, and our foe is the Devil.

Respect for principled living and the denial of selfish lusts are key to success, inwardly and outwardly.

Personally, I would prefer a duel with guns, arrows, or even swords; however, that is not how it is. Instead, it is wrestling, during which the Devil wraps around our minds, grips our bodies, and gets tangled up in our emotions. His purpose? To establish and reinforce strongholds anywhere he can.

A stronghold is a strong hold, a fortress for the Devil inside our thoughts. It is an entrenched thought pattern that keeps us in a way of life outside of God's will, a rut in our mind that we can't seem to get out of. There are a thousand of these plausible sounding arguments, all prompted by the Devil, that keep believers from living in the blessings and power of God. Satan paralyzes progress for God's kingdom with erroneous thoughts, and we must prepare for this warfare. We'll look at this in more detail in the next chapter.

WRESTLING WITH SELF

> *Where do wars and fights come from among you? Do they not come from your desires for pleasure that war in your members?* (James 4:1)

> *But I see another law in my members, warring against the law of my mind, and bringing me into captivity to the law of sin which is in my members. O wretched man that I am! Who will deliver me from this body of death? I thank God; through Jesus Christ our Lord! So then, with the mind I myself serve the law of God, but with the flesh the law of sin.* (Romans 7:23–25)

As these verses show, the making of a great leader starts with mastering the spirit. To conquer the person within is the personal Mount Everest we each face here on earth.

> *Whoever has no rule over his own spirit is like a city broken down, without walls.* (Proverbs 25:28)

Without rule over our inner self, we are defenseless against the attacks of the Devil. We become emotionally overwhelmed at every turn, and we are internally dysfunctional. Our *"city"* is broken down. The learning centers, the healing centers, the communications, the rubbish disposals, the government, the intelligence, the energy resources, orderliness—all break down from a failure to gain mastery of our spirits, our attitudes, our hearts. The Bible also reminds us that it is from our hearts that all the issues of life flow (Proverbs 4:23). Therefore, we must give due diligence to guard this sacred inner space of our lives.

> *He who is slow to anger is better than the mighty, and he who rules his spirit than he who takes a city.*
> (Proverbs 16:32)

Our capacity to achieve great results, to overwhelm powerful enemies, and to accomplish great dreams comes from the fact that we have gained mastery over our lives, harnessed our abilities, and made our behavior conform to a set of godly principles and directions. People who rule their spirits have obtained a power greater than one who can take a city.

The equation is obvious. If they've obtained a power greater than one who can take a city, they have also gained the capacity to "take a city." This is something God has called some leaders to do—to "take" a particular piece of the landscape for Him. There are certain people groups, certain projects, and certain events God wants us to "take." He selects leaders to do this. He selects those who have shown mastery over their own lives.

Many have thought self-mastery can be achieved in a day and then the matter would be settled, only to find themselves at the base of the mountain again the next day. Gaining mastery of our lives is an ongoing process, a continuing growth experience. Bringing our attitudes, thoughts, emotions, and speech under the lordship of Christ is a daily choice, but we have great keys to accomplish this victory.

It is essential for us as leaders to rule our spirits. If we are governed by our emotions, we have little chance of success. We will all be offended at times. People will do us wrong, and sometimes we will be treated like dirt. Right then is when we need to be bigger than our natural responses. Learning to love people we want to hate, forgiving people we want to resent, helping people who have hurt us, encouraging people who have discouraged us, and speaking well of those who have spoken evil against us are the tasks every great leader must undertake. Living by the principles of the kingdom of God is the foundation of leadership.

Truly great kingdom leaders are disciples of Christ. They are interested more in following Jesus than in leading people. They are more interested in pleasing God than in pleasing those they lead.

People who rule their spirits have obtained a power greater than one who can take a city.

Jesus told us, *"If anyone desires to come after Me, let him deny himself* [lay down his life], *and take up his cross daily, and follow Me"* (Luke 9:23). Our natural inclination is to lay down the cross and pick up right where we left off with our lives. But surrendering to Jesus means that we release our agenda and take on His. We forget our plans and accept His, no matter what they are.

Generally, God doesn't tell me what His plan is before I'm surrendered to Him. It's not a matter of surrendering to His will; I often don't know exactly what that is. I don't get the option to check out His will and then decide whether or not I'm going to be committed to serving the Lord. My surrender must be to Him alone, trusting that His will is not going to be grievous or burdensome (1 John 5:3) and that, with the psalmist, I can wholeheartedly say, *"I delight to do Your will"* (Psalm 40:8). I lay down the way I do things and take up His way of doing things. I let go of the results I want and accept the results He wants. This is where the struggle is. This is where we wrestle with ourselves. If we win this victory, we don't have to struggle with a thousand other issues.

WRESTLING WITH GOD

God wants to develop the highest degree of qualities in us, yet sometimes it seems God is hesitant to answer our prayers. This apparent initial reluctance is not a denial but a design to provoke our spirits to a more desperate, less complacent prayer encounter with the Almighty.

> *So Jacob was left alone, and a man wrestled with him till daybreak. When the man saw that he could not overpower him, he touched the socket of Jacob's hip so that his hip was wrenched as he wrestled with the man. Then the man said, "Let me go, for it is daybreak." But Jacob replied, "I will not let you go unless you bless me."* (Genesis 32:24–26 NIV)

There are crucial, defining moments in the life of every leader, especially developing leaders. At these points, it seems that God asks for more than we can deliver—or even want to deliver. There are times when we must wrestle with God for greater breakthroughs. There are times when His apparent reluctance is far from refusal, but rather the invitation for us to persist in seeking, knocking, and asking.

To illustrate the power of unrelenting prayer, Jesus presented the parable of a defenseless widow wearing out an unjust judge through her sheer persistence to obtain justice. (See Luke 18:3–5.) An unanswered prayer does not mean God is unwilling to fulfill our petitions. However, Jesus plainly showed that dogged persistence *("importunity"* KJV) brings answers.

It is never easy to ask a person for the same thing again after being refused, but this is the lesson of the story. Jesus was telling us that "unashamed barefacedness" gets the answer.

There are times when we must wrestle with God for greater breakthroughs.

To drive home His point, Jesus painted a picture of another determined person who overcame initial refusal. (See Luke 11:5–10.) A man approached his neighbor at midnight to borrow bread. He had run out, and some hungry, late-night travelers had just arrived at his house. Despite the possibility of disturbing his neighbors and waking the entire household, the man knocked loudly on the door, calling out for bread. He was refused and told to go away.

This is interesting because, although a close relationship with the Lord is essential, it is no guarantee of answered prayer. Faith and persistence gain the answers we are looking for. Jesus said that even though the neighbor was his friend, he wouldn't come to the door and meet his request. However, the man refused to be refused. He continued knocking until his request was satisfied. This is what Jesus was soliciting: prayer that doesn't give up. This is what a leader must be capable of. He or she must be able to "pray through"—wrestling with God for answers that do not seem to come easily.

Another Bible example is when Elijah "heard" the sound of rain after he had slain the 400 prophets of Baal on Mount Carmel (1 Kings 18:41). He realized that even though he had seen the vision and heard the sound, this was no guarantee it would come to pass, and so he interceded with prayer from deep within.

He thought that he had broken through, and so he sent his servant to check the horizon. Nothing! He went to powerful, groaning prayer again. Again he felt release, and again the servant scoured the horizon. Still nothing! Seven times this happened. Finally on the seventh search, his servant noticed a small cloud on the horizon of the ocean. Elijah had broken through. Soon the sky was black, and rain poured down in a deluge, breaking a three-and-a-half-year drought.

This is persistent, powerful, effective prayer, like the prayer of the Canaanite woman who approached Jesus to deliver her daughter from a demon (Matthew 15:22). Initially, Jesus ignored her, and His disciples pushed her away (v. 23). When He did finally acknowledge her presence—just barely—He denied her request (v. 24); then He insulted her as He again refused her, referring to her as a little dog (v. 26). Even so, she persisted through it all. Jesus called this *"great...faith"* (v. 28). What wrestles with God? Great faith!

Hebrews tells us, *"Come boldly to the throne of grace, that we may obtain mercy and find grace to help in time of need"* (Hebrews 4:16). It is difficult to be bold when you've done wrong, when you're feeling guilty and ashamed. It can be very challenging to approach the almighty throne of God with boldness, especially when you're in need of mercy.

Yet it is right here that we are called to come boldly so that we can find the grace and mercy we need. Boldness—not weak, timid attempts at trying to placate God—obtains the promises, for faith pleases God. Faith is bold, persistent, and positive in seeking results. Although self-deprecating attitudes sound impressively pious to others, they do nothing for God. God meets with people who are rejoicing (Isaiah 64:5), and He responds to faith. (See, for example, Mark 9:23 and John 11:40.)

Boldness—not weak, timid attempts at trying to placate God—obtains promises.

Even though the Devil was responsible for tormenting Job, this could not have happened without permission from God. Job knew this. He felt God was against him. However, he refused to forsake his pleading with the Lord: *"Though He slay me, yet will I trust Him. Even so, I will defend my own ways before Him"* (Job 13:15). Job stood his ground before the Lord and refused to abandon his trust in God or the fact that he was not deserving of the afflictions heaped upon him. He wrestled and reasoned with God.

God Himself invites us to *"Come now, and...reason"* with Him (Isaiah 1:18). He wants you to *"state your case, that you may be acquitted ["proved right"* NASB]*"* (Isaiah 43:26). Job entered some unsubstantiated areas before God in his appeals, yet the final outcome was that Job was shown to be a truly righteous man, with whom God was well pleased. He held his ground and wrestled his way to victory, in spite of the fact that life had not played fair. His latter days were even more blessed than when he began:

*Now the L*ORD *blessed the latter days of Job more than his beginning; for he had fourteen thousand sheep, six thousand camels, one thousand yoke of oxen, and one thousand female donkeys. He also had seven sons and three daughters. And he called the name of the first Jemimah, the name of the second Keziah, and the name of the third Keren-Happuch. In all the land were found no women so beautiful as the daughters of Job; and their father gave them an inheritance among their brothers. After this Job lived one hundred and forty years, and saw his children and grandchildren for four generations. So Job died, old and full of days.* (Job 42:12–17)

PERSECUTION

Public men must expect public criticism.
—Charles Spurgeon

Blessed are those who are persecuted for righteousness' sake, for theirs is the kingdom of heaven. Blessed are you when they revile and persecute you, and say all kinds of evil against you falsely for My sake. Rejoice and be exceedingly glad, for great is your reward in heaven, for so they persecuted the prophets who were before you. (Matthew 5:10–12)

Part of the leadership package is facing criticism. Stand in front of people, and they will find fault. Nobody surrenders his or her direction in life to another without an opinion. The leader must be reconciled to the fact that, at least at some stage, this is the life of a leader. We cannot afford to become so sensitive to criticism that it overwhelms us. This has caused the destruction of many good leaders.

In my first year as a young pastor, two women gave me an enormous amount of grief through gossip and back-biting. They were founding members and had given generously to the beginnings of the church, but they were unhappy with the direction in which we were traveling and were letting others in the congregation know about it. I found this to be a very upsetting situation. It worried me much more than it should have.

Part of the leadership package is facing criticism. Stand in front of people, and they will find fault.

Finally, the Lord said to me, *"Do not fret because of evildoers"* (Proverbs 24:19). My reply was, "But, Lord, they're Christians!" He said, "They're doing evil, aren't they?" I had to agree. "So, they are evildoers," He said. This amazed me. I also felt the Lord was showing me they were being motivated not only by their own attitudes, but also by demon forces, so I went to prayer and bound the Devil from over them. Almost immediately, their attitudes changed.

The *"spirit of antichrist"* (1 John 4:3 KJV) doesn't manifest just to oppose Jesus. That would be too obvious. The Devil is a subtle schemer. The way this spirit opposes Christ is to oppose all Christians who are in leadership. We must realize the spirit of antichrist opposes all of the manifestations of Jesus on the earth. The accusations and criticisms leveled by this spirit sound reasonable and plausible. However, the leader's task is to ensure that this accusing spirit fails in its endeavor to undermine God-ordained movements.

The destiny of anything ordained by God is inevitable and awesome victory, and we are called to be part of that victory, no matter what criticisms may come.

It is difficult to find a training course that teaches us how to cope with criticism, yet this is probably one of the most perplexing things to deal with, especially when it's public. Living for Christ is often harder than dying for Him. The media today has learned the art of assassinating people's characters while leaving them alive. In the pursuit of ratings, in the pursuit of another scoop, in the drive to expose another scandal, great effort goes into smearing the reputations of people who are sometimes innocent.

As Dale Carnegie has said,

Any fool can criticize, condemn, and complain—and most fools do—but it takes character and self-control to be understanding and forgiving.

Of the material I've read on this matter, I have found Charles Spurgeon to have some of the most prudent counsel for us regarding how to handle criticism. The following eight points cover his teaching on the subject:

1. "You must be able to bear criticism, or you are not fit to be at the head of the congregation; and you must let the critic go without reckoning him among your deadly foes, or you will prove yourself a mere weakling."

2. "Public men must expect public criticism."

3. "We cannot expect those to approve of us whom we condemn by our testimony against their favorite sins."

4. "A sensible friend who will unsparingly criticize you from week to week will be a far greater blessing to you than a thousand indiscriminating admirers, if you have

sense enough to bear his treatment and grace enough to be thankful for it."

5. "In almost all cases, it is the wisest course to let such things die a natural death. A great lie, if unnoticed, is like a big fish out of water—it dashes and plunges and beats itself to death in a short time."

6. "Your blameless life will be your best defense."

7. "Abstain from fighting your own battles, and in nine cases out of ten, your accusers will gain nothing by their malevolence but chagrin for themselves and contempt from others. To prosecute the slanderer is very seldom wise."

8. "Our best course is to defend our innocence by our silence and leave our reputation with God. Yet there are exceptions to this general rule. When distinct, definite, public charges are made against a man, he is bound to answer them, and answer them in the clearest and most open manner." [25]

Leaders discover the "secret place" in God where they can flee when the tongues of evil people wag against them. This refuge is the place where I privately and deeply know the truth and can rest before God, aware that He knows, too. This awareness is also the realization that truth always surfaces eventually. There is always justice—if not now, then later. To know quietly that you have done no wrong and are yet accused wrongly is a powerful place to stay. Don't rush to defend yourself. Silence can be the loudest proclamation of innocence.

TRIALS OF FAITH

Cars are put through grueling tests before they're released to the public. God also tests faith before it is trusted with great exploits.

Smith Wigglesworth, the great "Apostle of Faith" of the early nineteenth century, declared, "Great faith comes from great trials."[26]

"Abraham, the man of faith" (Galatians 3:9 NIV) remains as the greatest human example of faith we have.

> *By faith Abraham, when he was tested, offered up Isaac, and he who had received the promises offered up his only begotten son, of whom it was said, "In Isaac your seed shall be called," concluding that God was able to raise him up, even from the dead, from which he also received him in a figurative sense.*
> (Hebrews 11:17–19)

Leaders discover the "secret place" in God where they can flee when the evil tongues wag against them.

God tested Abraham in four areas:

1. **Allegiance:** Did Abraham love God above all else, especially his only beloved Isaac?

2. **Obedience:** Would Abraham do anything that God asked Him to do?

3. **Surrender:** Would Abraham withhold anything at all from the Lord?

4. **Faith:** Did Abraham believe God could raise Isaac from the dead?

Once we have faith, it will be tested. Unproven faith is no faith at all. We need no faith for what we can see and what we can do. We need faith for what we cannot see; we need faith for what we cannot do. Doubt is part of the process of faith.

When we encounter doubt, we have reached the boundaries of our faith. We lay hold of the promises of God, and faith grows.

Abraham had not always had great faith. His faith increased as he continued the journey through his life, giving God the glory. What was he giving God the glory for? His future. God had made promises to him! Abraham believed these promises. He acted on these promises. God needed to prove that He could entrust the birth of His nation Israel to this man. Would Abraham father a nation that Yahweh could call family? God had made promises to Abraham that this nation would come through his son Isaac.

Isaac's birth itself was an incredible miracle. He was the fruit of Abraham's faith in the incredible promise that he and his wife, Sarah, at ages 100 and 90 respectively, would have a child. This impossible event had taken place, and Isaac had grown up. Whatever his age at the time, Isaac understood what was going on when God required Abraham to sacrifice him as an offering. This became the most demanding and perplexing moment in Abraham's life. If he killed the lad, how would God's promise then take place? He had waited an entire century for this boy. He had desired with an ache few of us have ever felt.

To sacrifice Isaac meant ultimate surrender to the Almighty. Abraham lived in a day of no Bible, no Old or New Testament. There were no preachers, no church meetings, no Bible studies, no worship albums, no tape-of-the-month clubs, and no conferences to build his faith—just the revelation of the Lord coming to him in the stillness of the cool desert nights, the quiet knowing within his spirit. The voice of the Lord cut through all his emotions. He obeyed.

Abraham told his wife that he and the boy were going on a three-day journey. At the designated mountain, he told his servants to remain at the foothills. He told them that he and the boy were going further on to worship and then added, *"We will come back to you"* (Genesis 22:5). This was Abraham's first great statement of faith. It reveals that he firmly believed that, even though he was going to slay his son Isaac, God would raise him from the dead. Even though this is something Abraham had never heard of before, he could see no other way to carry out God's command and yet for God to remain true to His Word.

Once we have faith, it will be tested.
Unproven faith is no faith at all.

They ascended the mountain. Isaac asked, "Where's the sacrifice?" Abraham answered from his faith. He believed he would offer his son upon a fiery altar. He believed that Isaac was the sacrifice God had provided: *"God will provide for Himself the lamb for a burnt offering"* (v. 8). He also believed God was about to raise his boy from the dead. (See Hebrews 11:19.)

He slowly bound the boy with cords. Isaac resigned himself quietly to his father's purpose. Although he was old enough to resist and run, he didn't. He had never had reason to doubt his father's love. He submitted and was laid upon the altar.

Abraham unsheathed his knife and raised it to slay the young man, his son, when a voice sounded from above. It called him to a halt! God absolved Abraham from the action.

He had proven that his obedience and faith were completely surrendered to God—not to those around him or even to himself. Abraham's joy and praise burst out to God. Isaac climbed down from the altar. Suddenly, out of nowhere it seemed, there was a ram tangled in the bushes nearby. God had provided His sacrifice and had found His man.

Trials of faith touch us in our most vulnerable and sensitive areas. Faith grows strong through these tests. This is why James wrote, *"Consider it all joy...when you encounter various trials"* (James 1:2 NASB). Trials are the things that make us, not break us.

SIX

THE LEADER'S WEAPONS

We discussed in the last chapter how one of the trials we face as Christians is warfare with the Devil. In this chapter, we'll take a look at how we can be victorious in warfare.

OUR WEAPONS OF WARFARE

We don't have many weapons for spiritual warfare because those weapons that we do have are extremely effective: *"For the weapons of our warfare are not carnal but mighty in God for pulling down strongholds"* (2 Corinthians 10:4).

1. THE WILL

The first great weapon we have is our own will. This is enormously important in the battle against evil forces. If our will is not set against the Devil, we will never gain victory.

God has given each of us a will that is sovereign in our personal world. Heaven respects our choices, and God does not force us to do anything. That is why there is a Judgment Day. If we had no choices, how could there be a Judgment Day? If we had no choice, what would God be judging us for?

God has given each of us a will that is sovereign in our personal world.

The truth is that we always have a choice. We would like to be rid of the Devil and all the negatives, but we're resistant to changing our heart attitudes and exercising our wills. The Devil leaves us when we have determined he has to leave, when we are resolute that he can no longer have any place in our world, when we have determinedly set our wills against him.

> *Therefore submit to God. Resist the devil and he will flee from you.* (James 4:7)

There's little point in yelling yourself hoarse against the Devil if you really don't want to lose the fruit of his presence. If you have not resolved to get rid of the Devil, it is unlikely that he'll go.

As James 4:7 says, we must *first* surrender to God and *then* resist the Devil. This is the key to success in overcoming. Satan gains access through our rebellion against God. If we are disobedient to known revelation from the Father, we are vulnerable to the schemes of the Devil. When we choose to obey God, however, we discover the power that drives out demons easily.

Again, some would love to get rid of the Devil, but they really don't want to obey God either. Oppression is no fun, but the call to obey God can be really challenging. It comes down to choosing God's will. Only then can we set our will against the Devil—and overcome him.

2. THE WORD

The second great weapon we have is the Word of God. Most people fight the Devil with their own words, but the sword of the Spirit is the Word of God (Ephesians 6:17). As we saw earlier, Jesus didn't fight the Devil without the Word of God. He didn't resort to words not already in Scripture.

Even now in heaven, Jesus fights with it. In Revelation 1:16, He moves among the seven churches with the sword coming from His mouth. In the nineteenth chapter of Revelation, we read that Jesus will return to the earth, coming as *"The Word of God"* (v. 13), with the sword in His mouth (v. 15) to bring judgment on the nations. *"And the armies of heaven...followed Him"* (v. 14). All the armies of heaven back up the Word of God. Why do we imagine we could be successful any other way? Pick up your sword! It has been lying on the ground too long. Speak the Word of God!

The power of the Word is discovered in two realms. The general promises of Scripture are powerful, but there are also the personal words that God gives us over the years, Bible passages that He quickens or makes alive in our spirits passages that pertain especially to us. These *rhema* words, or utterings from God, are like manna in the pot that never decays (Exodus 16:33). These *rhema* words are always effective for building our faith and defeating the Devil. This is the *"two-edged sword"* of Hebrews 4:12.

The most effective weapon we have against Satan is the Word of God. We have a vast power in the Word. It lies untapped, though, until we pick it up. We need to continue to speak this Word of God against the Devil until we have overcome.

3. THE NAME

The third great weapon in our arsenal is the name of Jesus. This is the authority we have in Christ. If we have accepted Jesus Christ as Ruler of our lives, that rule travels through the whole of our lives.

In addition, we have His authority. Since we are conquerors with Him, we are no longer under the authority of sin and death.

We need to be careful, however, in how we treat the name of Jesus. It is not some magical formula we can use to get whatever we want. It is for spiritual warfare, and it is a name to be honored.

Demons throughout the celestial spiritual regions are fully aware of the person of Jesus. They realize that He has thoroughly defeated and humiliated their leader, that Jesus has crushed Satan in the dust of hell. They can do nothing except bow at the name of Jesus:

> *Therefore God also has highly exalted Him and given Him the name which is above every name, that at the name of Jesus every knee should bow, of those in heaven, and of those on earth, and of those under the earth.*
> (Philippians 2:9–10)

Throughout the book of Acts, we read how the early apostles discovered the power of that name to heal the sick, cast out devils, and raise the dead. The authority of Jesus' name declared by the Spirit-filled church brings down any devil on earth.

4. BINDING THE STRONGMAN

Embarking on fresh exploits for God almost always introduces the need to deal with demonic forces in a systematic way: *"Or how can one enter a strong man's house and plunder his goods, unless he first binds the strong man? And then he will plunder his house"* (Matthew 12:29).

Most people fight the Devil with their own words, but the sword of the Spirit is the Word of God.

Any leader setting out to accomplish something great will encounter opposition. Irrational catastrophes, evil thoughts, black emotions, terrible tragedies, and horrific conflicts are part of the long war with the powers of darkness. We cannot afford to ignore this fact; otherwise, we will never properly deal with the Devil. Recognize his work, rise up against the insidious schemer, exercise your will, and engage the Word of God in bold declaration of the name of Jesus. Be dangerous! The Devil will flee.

In 1989 I wrote a song called "Binding the Strongman." The song was birthed out of a powerful spiritual experience.

Our Christian City Church International Conference was being held at Collaroy Conference Center on the Northern Beaches of Sydney. A great servant of God from New Zealand, Peter Morrow, was speaking on the power of the Word of God at one of the sessions. As he spoke, I became aware of a demon crouching in front of me.

I am not given to seeing demons. This had never happened to me before and has never happened since in all my years of following Christ. But unmistakably there in front of me was a devil. It was in a "ready to pounce" stance, looking muscular and powerful, like a strong man. It appeared completely devoted to me. Like a sheepdog, it was watching my every motion, and it moved to block whatever forward action I tried to take. It did not take its eyes off me.

Under my breath, I told it to get out, but nothing happened. I kept doing this without any effect. I was sitting in the front row, listening to Peter's message, which happened, at that moment, to be about the power of the spoken Word. I realized there was a connection: I needed to speak the Word of God in this battle.

I asked myself what Scripture I should speak. The Lord quickened Romans 8:28 to my spirit: *"All things work together for good to those who love God, to those who are the called according to His purpose."* I thought, "That doesn't really sound like a great warfare Scripture." It sounded too pious for a fight with the Devil, but I started to repeat this verse anyway.

The first time, the demon simply sneezed, wiped its nose, and stared right back at me, resuming its sentry stance. I tried again, still with the same results. I got more determined. I kept speaking the Scripture—as aggressively as I could in the meeting—under my breath into the teeth of this demon. After twenty minutes or so, it seemed nothing much had changed. The only thing I was more aware of was that this was a demon devoted to hindering our progress as a church. Its focus was completely on me, and it was a strongman.

For about seven years, we had attempted to get a large block of land rezoned. In the long battle with the local government and residents, we had been defeated in our applications three times. National television shows had depicted us as a big wealthy Pentecostal group developing an international headquarters and theme park similar to that of Jim Bakker in the U.S. The local paper had run negative stories on us, and there were many other kinds of opposition.

The authority of Jesus' name declared by the Spirit-filled church brings down any devil on earth.

Morale in the church was pretty low at times during this season as well. Even though we have an unlisted home phone number, we had received several calls in the middle of the night from satanists telling us they were making sacrifices against us ever putting up our building. We would hear screaming and gurgling sounds over the phone. We realized we were involved in major warfare over that building. As I became aware that this demon was the strongman obstructing our progress, I became more determined than ever to bind it.

Peter finished preaching, and I closed the meeting. As soon as I could, I went to my room and continued praying. I immediately saw the demon again, but it was smaller, further away, and weaker. Its hands were hanging at its side. I prayed a little longer but didn't actually feel the need to. The job was done. As I went back to prayer later in the day, again I saw the demon. This time it was completely bound with chains wrapped all around it. It couldn't move in any way, even though it desperately struggled to. The Lord spoke to me right then. He said, "The Devil is bound. You have a clear run to the end."

Within a few weeks, the attitude of our local government and surrounding residents completely changed toward us. After some more lobbying with lawyers and design changes with the architects, we resubmitted our plans. They went through, completely unopposed by anybody. Amazing! We have since submitted two further plans for more buildings to complete the project, and all are going through without a hitch.

The state government has also installed—and paid for—the traffic lights required of us at the intersection adjacent to our property. That amounts to around $250,000. This is unheard of by developers in the area! Muslim contractors laying the tiles carried out their work at cost, donating $65,000 to the project. All together, the entire project has cost around $11 million and is already almost all paid for. God's Word is alive and well—and it works!

As the auditorium neared completion, I noticed the seating started about six feet from the stage. This concerned me. A lot of what we do in our church needs a larger than normal altar area. The Lord spoke to me, asking a question: "What are you building here?"

"A church building," I replied.

"No you're not. You're meant to be building an altar."

This awakened an entirely new perspective on many things to do with buildings and land for churches. I realized God had given us this small piece of the planet, and we were now erecting a great altar for Him. Here, people by the thousands would be offering their lives to God, getting saved, worshipping, praying, giving finances, preparing for service in our ministry training schools, and serving God in a thousand other ways. I relate this story because it then became obvious to me why the Devil had so vehemently opposed the entire exercise.

As we bind the strongman, we plunder his goods.

As we bind the strongman, we plunder his goods. Altars and sacrifices to God are powerful in transforming spiritual complexions and cultures in a city. The fire of God falls on sacrifices placed upon altars throughout Scripture. Thus, I wrote the song, "Binding the Strongman":

> We're binding the strongman,
> We're loosing the captives,
> We're slaying Goliath,
> We're setting the prisoners free.
> We're calling down fire,
> We're calling down fire,
> We're calling down fire from heaven.

There is an awesome power in the great Word of God. With the Word, we win the war against the Devil.

For we do not wrestle against flesh and blood, but against principalities, against powers, against the rulers of the darkness of this age, against spiritual hosts of wickedness in the heavenly places. Therefore take up the whole armor of God, that you may be able to withstand in the evil day, and having done all, to stand. Stand therefore, having girded your waist with truth, having put on the breastplate of righteousness, and having shod your feet with the preparation of the gospel of peace;

*above all, taking the shield of faith with which you will
be able to quench all the fiery darts of the wicked one.
And take the helmet of salvation, and the sword of the
Spirit, which is the word of God; praying always with
all prayer and supplication in the Spirit, being watch-
ful to this end with all perseverance and supplication
for all the saints.* (Ephesians 6:12–18)

Our battle is not with what we can see. Although we
argue, fight, and struggle with our physical world, we are
not just wrestling with this realm. Recognizing the Devil at
work is the first big step in defeating him.

5. Forgiveness

Generally, each of us has one or two vulnerable areas
that the Devil attacks consistently. For many people, unfor-
giveness is one of those targeted areas.

The apostle Paul told the Corinthians to forgive a certain person whom they had been disciplining so that the
Devil couldn't gain an advantage over the brother through
depression and rejection, or over themselves through unfor-
giveness. (See 2 Corinthians 2:6–11.) Practicing forgiveness
is a crucial weapon in our warfare with the Devil.

6. Authority in the Anointing

In the matter of spiritual warfare, people have specific
realms of responsibility. In a sense, we have specific authority
over specific territories. Moses held his rod to the sky, atop
a mountain overlooking the battle below between Israel and
the Amalekites. He grew tired. His helpers, Aaron and Hur,
supported his arms—but they didn't offer to hold the rod.
For them, it was never a matter of taking turns since God
had appointed Moses—not them—as the one with responsibility for the young Israelite nation. It was Moses' anointed

role, and he alone had the authority. Aaron and Hur simply supported him in exercising that authority.

As Moses held the rod high, Joshua led the army to victory. When Moses wearied and the rod dropped, the tide turned against the army below. Who would have thought that holding a rod in the air would make any difference? The truth is that the rod in anyone else's hand actually wouldn't have made a difference—but in Moses' hand, it released the power of God.

Although we struggle with our physical world, we are not just wrestling with this realm.

God anointed the man, and the man had a method—to use what was *"in* [his] *hand...a rod"* (Exodus 4:2). We must not be deluded into thinking that God has anointed techniques. Authority is given to people, not methods; God anoints people, not techniques. Only in the hands of an anointed person will a technique become successful and fruitful.

The kingdom leader knows how to beat the Devil. We must always remember that Satan can be beaten. Jesus has already done it, and now we share His victory: *"For You, LORD, have made me glad through Your work; I will triumph in the works of Your hands"* (Psalm 92:4).

seven

****

The Leader and His Attitude

****

Keep your heart [attitude] *with all diligence,*
for out of it spring the issues of life.
—Proverbs 4:23

Attitude is everything. In this verse from Proverbs, Solomon admonished us to guard our hearts, our inner attitudes, diligently because all the issues of life spring from that source.

Paul told us that faith, hope, and love are the best attitudes we can nurture within ourselves: *"And now these three remain: faith, hope and love"* (1 Corinthians 13:13 NIV). Certainly these are very powerful characteristics. Let me give you five others as well.

A Positive Attitude

In my view, a positive attitude is essential for bringing anything to pass. It is vital to see the upside of everything. We've all met people from the negative crowd; their views are cynical, suspicious, and depressing. Being positive about anything and everything, however, is the key to spotting opportunity and to brightening others around you. People are attracted to light; they are attracted to a positive view.

A Willing Attitude

Willingness is an enormous key to success in life. It's difficult to get unwilling personalities to do anything; they always have a reason why they can't do things.

I remember a story Kenneth Hagin told of when he was called away from pastoring a church to become a traveling evangelist. He said that he had no money, and as he drove along, his tires were so bald that they were all singing. Because he had obeyed God and launched out as an itinerant minister, he complained to the Lord that the promise of his eating *"the good of the land"* if he was *"willing and obedient"* (Isaiah 1:19) simply was not working. The Lord replied, "You're obedient, but you're not willing." Hagin said he got willing in about two seconds flat!

I love the "can-do" crowd. Success comes in a *can*—not a *cannot*! Working with a team of willing people is a dream. No problem is so big that can't be solved. No dream is impossible. Achievement often doesn't have a lot to do with faith, education, or talent, but everything to do with the simple attitude of willingness.

A Thankful Attitude

> Blow, blow, thou winter wind! Thou art not so unkind as man's ingratitude. [27]
> —William Shakespeare

The Bible tells us that the last days will be marked by unthankfulness (2 Timothy 3:2). Thankfulness anchors us so that we see everything from a positive, meaningful viewpoint. Thankful hearts please God and draw us close to Him. It is impossible to maintain a great attitude without a thankful heart.

Thankfulness triumphs over just being positive because it brings God and others into our bright view of life, and because it invokes a humble heart. On the other hand, there are times when being positive simply becomes cold, insensitive arrogance. If we're thankful, we acknowledge that it wasn't our prowess that accomplished anything. Thankfulness places credit where credit is due.

Thankfulness anchors us so that we see everything from a positive, meaningful viewpoint.

Although I've said this before, it bears repeating: Proverbs 16:32 indicates that people who have their spirits (attitudes) under control have the capacity to "take a city." This is because they have conquered the *"city"* within. We only accomplish outside what we have accomplished inside.

Leaders have learned to rule their attitudes. They are not waiting to see how they feel. They know how they want to feel and choose to "feel" that way. They do not live at the mercy of their emotions or moods. Their moods are the product of their choices, and they obey the command to *"rejoice always"* (1 Thessalonians 5:16). The New Testament has an abundance of commands relating directly to our attitudes. We choose to love, to be patient, to have faith, to be generous, and to forgive, even when our emotions want to do otherwise. We choose to lead ourselves. Thus, we become leaders—people who can take a city.

A JOYFUL ATTITUDE

A sense of humor is part of a great attitude. It begins by never taking yourself too seriously. Abraham Lincoln was known for his sober approach to life and leadership, yet he recognized the value of a merry heart: "Don't forget that humor is a major component of your ability to persuade people. A good laugh is good for both the mental and physical digestion." [28] Even Shirley MacLaine has been able to see the importance of laughter: "The person who knows how to laugh at himself will never cease to be amused."

I can't remember meeting a great leader yet who did not possess an equally great sense of humor. Humor reveals sanity. People more easily trust someone who is able to laugh at genuinely funny things than those who have outlawed any expressions of happiness from their emotions. Humor allows us to see the lighter side of life. This, in itself, is a relief from the pressures of leadership.

The jester in the court of the king is a metaphor of our need for a lighthearted state of mind. I believe the atmosphere around a home, a church, a business, or any organization is a reflection of its leadership. If the atmosphere is intense and heavy, people won't develop and grow. They are restrained from freely expressing themselves. In a lighter atmosphere, however, people are far freer to welcome others, to express themselves, and to rejoice. This comes when leaders recognize the need to lighten up.

The Sydney newspaper *The Daily Telegraph* recently posted an article, "Fun Keeps You Fit," on the benefits of laughter:

> Hundreds of medical research papers have shown that fun keeps you fit. A good old guffaw acts as a sort of internal aerobics, working the muscles of the heart and upper body, stimulating the nerves and improving the way the body uses oxygen.
>
> Laughter lowers blood pressure and massages the heart, lungs and other vital organs. A baby's first chuckle emerges around three months. By age six, it laughs about 300 times a day, by adulthood, around 47 times a day—100 for the most cheerful.
>
> Laughter triggers the release of an antibody called immuno-globin A, which boosts the immune system. Even if you do become ill, a good chuckle speeds the healing process. People so serious about cholesterol levels, strict diets, and a seriously healthier lifestyle would do better to have a bit more fun and laugh a whole lot more alongside of living healthier.
>
> Dr. Renshaw, associate to Ben Holden, who set up a National Health Service Laughter Clinic in 1991 (in Britain), also says, "The people who live the longest and stay healthiest are those who are the happiest and most creative."
>
> A Mr. Norman was suffering from an incurable disease and to brighten his days began watching Marx Brothers movies. The pleasure of one film gave him two pain free hours of sleep. He checked himself out of the hospital room into a hotel room where he laughed himself back to health....

++

Women smile more than men, especially when they are doing the talking. Women laugh a lot more than men when talking to another person.

Playfulness is an art never to be lost. It is said we do not stop playing because we get old. We get old because we stop playing.

If others are laughing, laugh along with them. Let it catch you. Get infected. [29]

Although the article claimed Norman Cousins as the pioneer of mirth as medicine, the Bible has always contained this verse: *"A merry heart does good, like medicine, but a broken spirit dries the bones"* (Proverbs 17:22).

++

A sense of humor is part of a great attitude. It begins by never taking yourself too seriously.

++

Even St. Francis of Assisi, the mystic invariably portrayed as a dour-faced devotee, saw the value of mirth: "When we who are servants of Christ stand in the center of the Devil's cloud of doubt and accusation and, instead of breathing this choking dust, refresh ourselves in the water of God's joy until it overflows even in holy laughter—then not a single demon can harm us in any way." [30]

Postponing joy until something happens to justify happiness guarantees a miserable life. Joy is within right now.

A MOTIVATED ATTITUDE

Motivation is an attitude—it's a spirit of continual enthusiasm. Motivation is an attitude of going for it. "Let's make things happen!" is how leaders think. Leaders don't wait to see what will happen; they make things happen.

Too often, followers just sit on the sidelines, waiting to see what's going to happen. If we believe in an idea, then we need to make it happen. If we don't believe in something, then we shouldn't get involved in it. The word *enthusiasm* in its original sense means being filled with a passion for God.

Postponing joy until something happens to justify happiness guarantees a miserable life.

Motivation comes easily at the beginning of an idea. A great idea is a powerful motivator. However, the initial idea is only the beginning of the journey. It's only about ten percent of the entire process of bringing a dream to pass. Distractions, laziness, and discouragement are three serious enemies to continual motivation.

Maintaining motivation is a daily commitment. We must understand what gets us going. What starts me? What keeps me going? What will keep the team energized? There are positive motivators and negative motivators. Both can be effective in keeping us moving. It takes time and energy—generally much more than we anticipated— to go the full course and fulfill the dream. Visions always take longer than we want. Different things motivate us at different times during the journey.

The most powerful motivator of all is commitment. The will is amazingly strong. Once we've decided to do a thing, we release a power within that drives us on. Trying to accomplish something without really making the decision we're going to do it blocks energy, creativity, and resources that combine to bring the dream to pass. Instead, we need to stick with our decision until we reach the goal.

In order to keep ourselves in the "can-do" and "do-it-now" attitude, we have to continually fill our motivation tank with all the motivators we can lay our hands on. Surrounding ourselves with positive people who believe in what we're doing and who encourage us fills the motivation tank.

Listening to great communicators moves us. We have such an incredible opportunity these days with the books and tapes available to us. We can sit down with the greatest achievers and the greatest minds of history. We can have them speak to us in areas where they are experts, in a private one-on-one meeting. Through this material we motivate ourselves to achieve at ever higher levels.

Music is a powerful motivator. I regularly listen to great music, especially praise and worship to God. This always lifts my spirit. Even if I am not in the mood, I get myself into a God-focused state by letting the power of great praise and worship do its work on my soul.

I learn about the achievements of others in my own age bracket and those of a similar standing. This always gets me moving. When I see what others are doing, it stirs the possibilities within me. The mere feeling of competition motivates me to higher levels.

I personally have no problem with this, although some may. I believe in friendly competition with a great attitude and in playing by the rules. Certainly Paul employed this principle when he told the Jewish people all that God was doing among the Gentiles, hoping to motivate them with envy. (See Romans 11:14.) He spoke to the Corinthians of the abundantly generous pledge of the Macedonians, and vice versa, so they were motivated to achieve similar results. (See 2 Corinthians 8:1 and 9:2.)

eight

***

The Leader Is a Shepherd

***

Leadership is all about God and people.

A leader must serve as a shepherd for the people he or she leads. No matter what area of leadership we're in, we must have the heart of shepherds. Whether I'm the deacon's leader or the choir leader, the CEO of a company or the supervisor of a department, a prerequisite for my role is that, as a Christian, I care for the people. I'm not in leadership for the power, the prestige, or the rewards. I'm there because I care for people. I have the heart of the Father pulsing within me.

People matter to God—lost people and found people. Over the decades that I've known my good friend Frank Houston, pastor of one of Australia's greatest churches, he has repeatedly said regarding church leadership, "Ministry is all about God and people." If we as leaders are not interested in people, we are badly prepared for leadership. When people matter to us, other things we thought mattered more fade in importance. Leadership is all about people, people, and people.

A congregation very quickly discerns whether the pastor loves them or the ministry more. The same holds true for business leaders and their employees. Are they trying to impress, or do they genuinely care for the people? Are they preserving power, seeking rewards and prestige, or are they there for people? Jesus told us that the difference becomes crystal clear in the face of danger. Hirelings will flee when danger approaches because they care more for themselves than for the sheep. Shepherds, however, stay, fight, and even lay down their lives for the sheep. (See John 10:11–13.)

People matter to God— lost people and found people.

In my realm of leadership, occasionally I have met ministers who refer to their churches as bases for their ministries. To me, this is faulty thinking. This kind of philosophy is one that promotes using the home church as a springboard to something the minister imagines is more important. People are not a base. They are people—God's people. If we think that our church is a platform for our ministry, then we are asking the people to lay down their lives for the shepherd. This is not the biblical model. The shepherd lays down his life for the sheep, not the other way around.

In this chapter, we'll take a look at how the leader must serve as a shepherd. Perhaps one of the best examples of shepherd leadership is found in the church, where pastors look after their congregational flocks. In examining how successful pastors shepherd their flocks, we can learn principles that apply to all leadership positions.

A Shepherd's Tasks in the Church

Shepherds accomplish many things in church life for the flocks they have been given to care for. Here are some of the major things shepherd need to provide in order for their flocks to grow.

Open Doors

One very big part the shepherd plays is opening the doors of the church. Shepherds must let people "in." It is one thing to get people to sign up as members but quite another to let them "own" the church—to let them take on roles and responsibilities. The old guard resists this concept, holding on to their sphere of power and influence. Yet the key to church growth is to let the people know the church is theirs.

When newcomers turn up, they always have a bundle of ideas and stuff they're carrying from wherever they've been. A smart leader isn't quick to correct newcomers and make them conform to their new environs. Give people room to "buy in" to the new culture that attracted them in the first place. Their previously held beliefs provide them security. Don't rip that security away from them. Allow people time to embrace the new; then they will discard the old.

This is a kingdom principle. The merchant who was searching for the pearl of great price sold all that he owned only when he had found the treasure he had been looking for (Matthew 13:46).

Presence

The shepherd is a "there" person. Presence is important. In the shepherd's absence, the sheep worry and get restless.

Just being visible, present, and sensed provides a stable, secure environment. Sheep without a shepherd become fatigued and misdirected, weary and scattered. It has always fascinated me that the friends of Job simply sat with him for seven days, without saying a word (Job 2:13). Being there is comfort enough in many situations.

PROMPTNESS

A good shepherd attends to people's problems quickly. The shepherd is always there in a crisis or a great life-moment. The minute you know someone has died, drop everything else to be with the family. The moment you're aware of a tragedy, be there. Not only do we need to attend to problems, we need to be effective in solving them. Great leaders are great problem solvers for individuals and for groups.

GUIDANCE

Good shepherding gives people guidance that is simple and clear in all areas of their lives. Some leaders are so confused themselves that they can't guide anyone else. The art of guiding involves helping people discover the will of God. This guidance is generally already within people. Bringing them to the point where they can discern and understand the will of God is often simply a matter of asking questions that lead them to a consciousness of what is already in their spirits. When we create an environment of empathy, we draw out the counsel of God hidden in the hearts of the people we are guiding.

> *Counsel in the heart of man is like deep water, but a man of understanding will draw it out.*
>
> (Proverbs 20:5)

Listening is a large part of bringing guidance to people. If people know they are being heard, if they know that someone is listening and cares about what they are saying, they will often arrive at their own answers.

The art of guiding involves helping people discover the will of God.

The shepherd needs to have guiding input with matters that involve major decisions in the life of his or her people. An overseer has oversight—he or she sees from above. Anyone who has the higher ground has the advantage and is able to show people the way through the maze.

Too many believers have entered into partnerships, deals, and major decisions without some input, even if just in prayer, from their pastor. Many times I've seen believers make foolish decisions that have robbed them of their finances or their security simply because they have not had the guidance of a pastor. Of course, people have to want to be guided and to be willing to accept outside input. That's essential. I've also seen a lot of people ignore sound guidance at their own peril.

PROTECTION FROM ENEMIES

True shepherds don't flee when there's trouble. We stay at our posts. We work it out. This means shepherds defeat the enemies of God's people. We're effective in casting out the Devil and overthrowing his attacks on the saints. We defeat false doctrines trying to lure saints away from Christ. We guide our people away from infectious fellowship.

Backsliders, or Christians living wrongly, don't help believers at all. They can infect good people with spiritual diseases. Our role keeps the people of God free from teachings and people that could corrupt them. Good shepherding keeps the people of God in God and out of the world. Godly leaders protect their churches from worldliness without becoming legalistic, so that people discover the joy and beauty of holiness rather than imagining they have to keep an impossible set of rules.

Zealotry can be just as dangerous as backsliding.

We should also keep our people from zealotry. This is just as dangerous as backsliding. People who become Christian zealots are a pain to everyone. They alienate people from God. They criticize the church because it is never on fire enough, or godly enough, or whatever. Generally, they burn out in a short time because the "fire" they're lit with cannot be sustained. Sincere believers can be seduced by the idealism of these people, and left burned and broken when the whole affair falls apart. C. S. Lewis alludes to this in *The Screwtape Letters* when the demons are designing their schemes against humankind. The basic ploy is that, if they cannot get Christians to be lukewarm or backslidden, they will attempt to make them fanatics. [31]

SECURITY

An experience I will always treasure is that of our children falling asleep in my arms. This is complete trust. Their level of trust is high because, as their dad, I have supplied not only the basic necessities of life—food, clothing, and shelter—but also the intangibles such as guidance, boundaries, and protection. I was there physically and emotionally to fall asleep on. Because children are trusting by nature, they will also fall asleep in a stranger's arms. Yet if that adult is nervous or insecure, the child senses it. Sleep comes hard or fitfully, and the child squirms. A calm, confident leader provides a climate in which the children of God can sense safety. In that secure environment, they can rest in the house of the Lord.

NOURISHMENT

The shepherd must feed God's people. In the church, this means that the shepherd regularly imparts revelation from the Word of God, feeding the spirit of God's people. A church feeding on the revelation of the Word of God will be a powerful, fruitful assembly of believers who achieve amazing things for God. The faithful minister consistently feeds the flock tender green grass from the Word of God. This is food for the saints. It is easily digested. And this can only be accomplished when the leader spends time in study, gaining anointing and revelation. Through anointed preaching, the people are spiritually nourished and content. They will *"lie down in* [the] *green pastures"* (Psalm 23:2) of the church.

I consider the preaching of the Word to be the primary call on my life as a pastor—not administration or management or counseling, but feeding the flock the Word of God. I set aside at least one-and-a-half days a week to prepare for Sunday's meetings. Feeding the flock is the top priority for any pastor. If a pastor is too busy for that, then that pastor is simply too busy. We must all attend to our primary calling more fully.

And the Lord said, "Who then is that faithful and wise steward, whom his master will make ruler over his household, to give them their portion of food in due season?" (Luke 12:42)

Pastors who have growing churches are sometimes accused of "stealing sheep" from other churches. However, rather than stealing, they have just provided green grass in a restful climate. If a preacher is not searching out the Word of God with a personal hunger and excitement, that pastor shouldn't be surprised when people find that the grass really is greener on the other side of the fence. It is essential that all pastors spend time in the Word and in the anointing—for themselves and for their flocks.

Leaders are intended to nurture those they lead, to care for their flocks as shepherds care for their sheep.

This same principle applies to all leaders. Whether it's in the church, the business, or the home, leaders are responsible for nurturing their flocks. For the business leader, this could mean allowing employees to attend seminars, financially providing for additional education, or simply complimenting them on a job well done. In the home, this nurturing spirit is visible in the mother who takes time to help her son with his math homework, or the father who cheers his daughter on in her soccer games each week.

No matter what the realm, leaders are intended to nurture those they lead, to care for their flocks as shepherds care for their sheep.

nine

****

THE LEADER IS A
PROBLEM SOLVER

****

There's always a way.

The will of God is never without problems. A vision from the Holy Spirit always carries with it immense challenges. There are times when it seems more like a nightmare than a blessing. However, leaders not only know *how* to solve problems; they *do* solve them.

First, leaders have faith in God that somehow, some way, He will show the way through. Leaders don't run from the problem. They attack it. There's always a way. Leaders believe that they can solve the problem somehow. Leaders are systematic, methodical, and persistent. Leaders keep going until they have broken through and arrived at the solution.

Thomas Alva Edison, the man responsible for the light bulb said, "I failed my way to success." [32] He often repeated an experiment several hundred times before actually inventing something. He became a genius by relentlessly developing his latent potential, by waking the sleeping genius within.

One of the quickest ways to gain leadership is to solve other people's problems. Just ask Jephthah. (See Judges 11:1–33.) He was an outcast, rejected from his family by his half-brothers. Why? He was the son of a harlot. Gilead had fathered all the boys, but Jephthah was illegitimate because his mother was not Gilead's wife. The half-siblings were unhappy about sharing the inheritance with this outsider, so they threw him out.

Jephthah went out into the desert and formed his own private army. He held patriotic feelings for Israel. He attacked and destroyed her enemies with his little band of outcasts. Then the people asked him to lead the entire nation. An outcast, the son of a harlot, became the acting "prime minister" of Israel. For the rest of his life, Jephthah could have hung his head and felt that all his opportunities were dried up, but he solved the problems his nation was facing. It was the foundation for his leadership.

The problem is never the problem; the real problem is our attitude toward it.

A problem solver is the most useful person around because most people don't know what to do with their problems. Most think their problems are their problems, but this is never the case. The problem is never the problem; the real problem is our attitude toward it.

Just ask David. Better still, ask his brothers, who were paralyzed with fear for six weeks by the taunts of a giant.

They were held captive by their own distorted perception to the point that they couldn't solve the problem. The giant was too big. They shivered in terror. But from David's perspective, formed by an absolute faith in God, the giant was simply too big to miss!

Your problem is your opportunity. The trouble with opportunities, however, is that they never come with labels. When opportunity knocks, the pessimist complains about the noise, but the faith person always sees a way through. The willing attitude always finds a way. The person of faith knows there's an answer, always, no matter how difficult the problem.

In the ninth chapter of John, we read of the time when Jesus met a beggar who had been born blind. The disciples asked Jesus whose fault it was that he suffered this blindness— his parents or the man himself? How ridiculous we become in searching for answers within the problem. "How much sin can a man accomplish inside his mother's womb, before he is born?" Jesus asked them. He let them know it wasn't a matter of finding out why, but a matter of solving the problem. He explained that the problem existed so the glory of God could be revealed.

That's the ultimate purpose of problems: to be solved by the power of God so His glory can be revealed. When God solves a problem, we see His glory in action. The problems we face can seem impossible, but that's where we find God. He is able to make all things possible. He made a way through the Red Sea for an entire nation. He defeated the Egyptian army through the power of a rod lifted in the sky. He raised the dead.

He changes people's lives. When men and women are bold and brave and step out to solve problems, the great power of

God begins to move with them to bring the miraculous into play. Thus the problem is solved.

People have a large array of problems. There are also a great variety of solutions. Here are some basic guidelines in problem solving:

❖ Gather all the information you can.

❖ Gather all the people involved and huddle.

❖ Communicate with everyone.

❖ The greater the problem, the greater the need for communication. Things get solved better in the light.

❖ Create faith that the problem can be solved.

❖ Foster a "can-do" attitude.

❖ Keep a cool head and a disciplined tongue.

❖ Don't let emotions rule the day.

❖ Warm heart, cool head; don't get this the wrong way around.

❖ Hear all sides of a problem before reaching conclusions.

❖ Stay humble; arrogance creates more problems.

❖ Anger solves nothing (James 1:20).

❖ Don't be in a rush to solve anything.

❖ Hasty decisions are generally bad ones.

❖ Gain counsel from experts.

Even a pesky insect can force a great answer so that we actually arrive at a better place after dealing with the problems it created. Back when cotton was "king" in the South, the boll weevil migrated from Mexico to the United States, destroying most of the cotton crops. Farmers were forced to grow a variety of crops such as corn, soybeans, and especially peanuts, and they learned to use their land to raise cattle, hogs, and chickens.

As a result, many farmers became more prosperous than in the days when their only crop grown was cotton. The people of Enterprise, Alabama, were so grateful for what had occurred that in 1919 they erected a monument to the boll weevil. When they turned from the single-crop system to diversified farming, they became wealthier. The inscription on the monument reads, "In profound appreciation of the boll weevil and what it has done as the herald of prosperity." [33]

ten

THE LEADER'S BIG THREE

The virtues of men are of more consequence to society than their
abilities; and for this reason, the heart should be cultivated
with more assiduity than the head. [34]
—*Noah Webster*

Great leaders are virtuous people. In order to be effective, leaders need to have righteous character qualities—or old-fashioned virtues—ingrained in their hearts and evident in their lives.

The word *virtue* is variously defined by *Merriam-Webster's Collegiate Dictionary, Eleventh Edition,* as "conformity to a standard of right, morality; a particular moral excellence; a commendable quality or trait, merit; a beneficial quality or power of a thing; purity in conduct and intention, chastity; manly strength or courage, valor; and a capacity to act, potency." People need to develop all of these facets of character in order to be great leaders.

Three essential, cardinal virtues of great leaders are wisdom, courage, and strength:

❖ Wisdom is the ability to discern right from wrong, to know the right thing to do in any situation.

❖ Courage is doing what is right, no matter what the consequences.

❖ Strength is the capacity to continue doing the right thing, to carry through to the end, to finish what you started.

WISDOM

Fear God and keep His commandments.
—Ecclesiastes 12:13

The books of Proverbs and Ecclesiastes were written by leaders to leaders. Much of it was actually authored by Solomon, who wrote of the instructions his father, David, had given him on the principles of godly living and leadership. The wisdom books in the Bible conclude that the height of wisdom is to *"fear God and keep His commandments"* (Ecclesiastes 12:13).

The fear of God motivates us to do right regardless of who knows, because we realize that, in the end, God knows. The fear of God means recognizing that God punishes sin. It recognizes that eventually every hidden act will come to light and receive due justice. It realizes that whatever we sow, we reap. It knows that God is the Ruler of all and that we, His creatures, are formed to do His will.

There are a number of qualities that combine to form the foundation of wisdom in a person.

LEARNING

For me the most surprising quality of wisdom is the capacity to learn. In my younger, more naïve years, I imagined that if we were wise, we would not need to gain any more knowledge or learn anything else. However, it became plain to me that the wise recognize that they *do not* know everything but are actually in need of gaining much more knowledge.

The fear of God motivates us to do right regardless of who knows.

The trademark of fools is that they are wise in their own eyes. The paradox for the wise is they do not think they are wise; therefore, they have a hunger to learn and to increase their knowledge and understanding. This is what wisdom is all about.

> *A wise man will hear and increase learning, and a man of understanding will attain wise counsel.*
>
> (Proverbs 1:5)

Geoffrey Kells, who at one time was the managing director of CSR Limited in Australia, lists learning, which he calls "continuous improvement," as one of the seven key ingredients in the making of a leader:

> In CSR we have our own definition of a leader. When you use the word *leader*, I think of it in terms of seven behaviors:
>
> 1. Clearing the way
> 2. Managing the business effectively

3. Inspiring through vision
4. Working through teams
5. Being personally customer focused
6. Participating in continuous improvement
7. Empowering people [35]

Self-initiated growth is vital. Growth never takes place without the capacity to learn. Learning comes from an attitude. The attitude of a great leader is "I want to learn." We never reach the point where we don't need to learn.

Give instruction to a wise man, and he will be still wiser; teach a just man, and he will increase in learning. (Proverbs 9:9)

As Henry Ford said,

Anyone who stops learning is old, whether at twenty or eighty. Anyone who keeps learning stays young. The greatest thing in life is to keep your mind young. [36]

This is why leaders are readers. The great leader never stops reading.

**Not all readers become leaders.
But all leaders must be readers.** [37]
—Harry S. Truman

Leaders devour everything they lay their hands on, especially biographies. Great leaders know they have never "arrived."

Leaders also know they have not yet done all they can do. They realize they don't know it all. In fact, the older they get, the more they realize how little they know. They recognize the need to grow and to change.

If the leader is personally growing, the organization he or she leads is growing. Jack Welch, the extraordinary CEO of General Electric, said, "Our behavior is driven by a fundamental core belief: the desire, and the ability, of an organization to continually learn from any source, anywhere—and to rapidly convert this learning into action—is its ultimate competitive advantage." [38]

FLEXIBILITY

Wisdom also requires flexibility. Wise leaders are not so rigid in the way they do things that they cannot change.

There is an abundance of material on varying styles of leadership. There are times in the life of any leader that every one of those styles will be relevant. Some material says the days of autocratic leadership are over and the days of relational leadership have arrived. I actually agree with this, but there are definitely times when a leader has to stand alone, make his or her requirements clearly known, and expect nothing less than prompt compliance.

Wise leaders are not so rigid in the way they do things that they cannot change.

Much of the time, a wise leader operates in a consensus style of leadership where he or she gleans the thoughts of the key players and then fashions those thoughts into a well-orchestrated plan that can be implemented. Everyone on the team can identify with the part he or she actually played in the creation of the plan. They can "own" the action. They can rightly say, "We came up with this plan, and I contributed this part." The leader who wins the hearts and souls of team members is wise. (See Proverbs 11:30.)

The great leader also understands pacing. There are times to move fast and there are times to move slowly. The wise leader knows that *"to everything there is a season, a time for every purpose under heaven"* (Ecclesiastes 3:1).

Flexibility is the capacity to switch attention, adjust emotional tone, and change direction with ease. Many people become so fixated on what they are doing that they find it very difficult to make adjustments or change direction when they need to. We must be able to go from a feisty board meeting to a gentle counseling session without letting one affect the other.

**None are so blind as visionaries;
we become myopic with vision.**

Leaders are especially prone to such intense focus that they find it difficult to do anything else. I have often said none are so blind as visionaries; we become myopic with vision. We need to be focused, but we cannot afford to exclude other opinions, different methods, and new directions.

Even when God has led us into some great territory, we must be aware that He will continue to move on. If we become stuck where God has led us in the past, we become stagnant. The river of God is a moving, progressive force. When we single out certain concepts, cultures, songs, or structures and circle around them again and again, we will eventually die.

Whatever lives, grows and moves. When we stop moving, we die. Moving means change. The progressive leader must have this ability. He or she must be open to new ideas. In fact, true leaders grow tired of the old and seek the new. None of the great leaders I've ever met is satisfied with the status quo. They seek change.

Personality profilers tell us that about three percent of the general population are potential leaders, people who seek and enjoy change and new things. However, sixty percent are the stable kind of people who resist change and seek security, predictability, and safety. This means leaders must be wise in application of their directions. *Change* is a dangerous word to most of the population. Words like *development*, *growth*, and *progress* are always better terms to lead with.

MODERATION

Do not be overly righteous, nor be overly wise: Why should you destroy yourself? Do not be overly wicked, nor be foolish: Why should you die before your time?
(Ecclesiastes 7:16–17)

The wise leader avoids extremes. Overcorrection is a problem racecar drivers and trapeze artists need to avoid if they are to survive. Fanatics, however, go beyond what is appropriate. They show signs of obsession.

The worst kind of fanatics are religious zealots. Their misdirected fervor condemns all who fail to subscribe to their rigid positions. They demand abnormal lifestyles and abandon good sense in the name of devotion. The sincere are easy prey for these wolves seeking power, advantage, or simply more people to justify their particular brand of madness.

Balance is too important for leaders to ignore. In *Secrets of Super Achievers*, Philip Baker has noted, "Most prime ministers and presidents are voted in on their strengths and lose on their weaknesses." [39]

Being *"tossed to and fro and carried about with every wind of doctrine"* (Ephesians 4:14) or blindly accepting every new idea that comes along reveals immaturity and a lack of discernment, especially for leaders. We can take hold of the new emphasis that God wants to impress on the church or on a community, but that doesn't mean we abandon the basics. We stay with the big picture.

Like a racecar driver or a trapeze artist, the wise leader avoids extremes and overcorrection.

On the other hand, we shouldn't go to the opposite extreme and become reactionaries, either. When a particular teaching comes forth, it is just as foolish to automatically denounce it simply because it differs from what we have been accustomed to. When Kenneth Copeland began preaching on prosperity, it seemed out of balance to many. Maybe it was, but few prophetic messages come forth as balanced thoughts. God often has to push the pendulum to the opposite side to get us back in balance. However, for whatever reasons, a lot of preachers took up arms against Copeland and began preaching against his message.

I have a simple philosophy of "rolling with the punches." This takes the heat out of a lot of the punches we take. I simply rolled with what a lot of others thought was a threat to the local church. In fact, we had Brother Copeland come twice and preach in our church. We've only ever been blessed by the message. If there are any extremes, we as leaders are able to address them and graciously bring whatever balance we feel is needed. However, we need to be careful that we don't throw the baby out with the bathwater.

INTEGRITY

Wisdom guides leaders to walking in integrity.

The integrity of the upright will guide them, but the perversity of the unfaithful will destroy them.

(Proverbs 11:3)

According to John Maxwell, "The dictionary defines *integrity* as 'the state of being complete, unified.' When I have integrity, my words and my deeds match. I am who I am, no matter where I am or who I am with."[40]

When an individual's internal and external behaviors and beliefs are consistent with each other, he or she is a person of integrity.

❖ Integrity is doing right when no one else is looking.

❖ Integrity is keeping promises.

❖ Integrity is being true to principles, regardless of consequences.

❖ Integrity is being faithful to the truth when it is uncomfortable, inconvenient, and personally costly.

❖ Integrity is consistently living righteous lives because we wish to please God.

People of integrity stand on solid ground. There are no skeletons in the closet that can come out to destroy them.

A person of integrity has a clear conscience. As Bert-Olof Svanholm, the former president and CEO of ASEA Brown-Boveri, said,

> **You should have a cool brain, a warm heart, and clean hands. If you succeed in that, then I think you are quite a good leader.** [41]

In *Developing the Leader within You,* John Maxwell stated,

> A person with integrity does not have divided loyalties (that's duplicity), nor is he or she merely pretending (that's hypocrisy). People with integrity are "whole" people; they can be identified by their single-mindedness. People with integrity have nothing to hide and nothing to fear. Their lives are open books. V. Gilbert Beers says, "A person of integrity is one who has established a system of values against which all of life is judged....Too often we try to be a 'human doing' before we have become a 'human being.' To earn trust a leader has to be authentic." [42]

Or, as Socrates said, "The first key to greatness is to be in reality what we appear to be." The more credible we are, the more confidence people place in us, thereby allowing us the privilege of influencing their lives. The less credible we are, the less confidence people place in us and the more quickly we lose our position and leadership.

Everything rises and falls on leadership, and leadership functions on the basis of trust. Consider what Dwight D. Eisenhower had to say on the subject:

> In order to be a leader, a man must have followers. And to have followers, a man must have their confidence. Hence, the supreme quality for a leader is

unquestionably integrity. Without it, no real success is possible, no matter whether it is on a section gang, a football field, in an army, or in an office. If a man's associates find that he lacks forthright integrity, he will fail. His teachings and actions must square with each other. The first great need, therefore, is integrity and high purpose. [43]

In the early 1800s, a Jewish lad was growing up in a small town in Germany. He came from a long line of rabbis on both sides of his family. His uncle was the chief rabbi in the town synagogue, where his family attended services together. When he was six years old, however, the boy's father, whom he greatly admired, decided that the family was now going to abandon their Jewish traditions and be baptized in the Lutheran church so he could continue his rather lucrative career as a lawyer in the midst of the growing hostility and discrimination against Jews. Stunned and confused, the young lad must have experienced a profound disappointment with the father whom he so esteemed, which turned into anger and a deep *"root of bitterness"* (Hebrews 12:15) that became evident in his adult life.

"In order to be a leader, a man must have followers."

After completing his formal education, he left Germany and began to write a book in which "he introduced a whole new worldview and conceived a movement that was designed to change the world. He described religion as 'the opiate for the masses.' He committed the people who followed him to life without God. His ideas became the norm for the governments for almost half the world's people. His name? Karl Marx, the father of the Communist movement. The history of the twentieth century, and perhaps beyond, was significantly affected because one father let his values become distorted."[44]

Life is like a vice; at times it will squeeze us. At those moments of pressure, whatever is inside will be found out. We cannot give what we do not have.

Image promises much but produces little. Integrity, however, never disappoints. For me, integrity means living it myself before leading others to live it.

Great lives are built on great personal integrity. Many people believe the "show must go on" even though they are dying inside with guilt and shame over an inner life that doesn't match their public display.

Effective leadership is not based on being clever but primarily on being consistent.

Effective leadership is not based on being clever. It is based primarily on being consistent. The only way to keep the goodwill and high esteem of the people you work with is to deserve it.

In 1987, the federal government conducted a major sting operation in New York to uncover money that had been illegally obtained by state public officials, 106 of whom were under investigation by the U.S. Attorney General's office. Afterward, Rudolph Giuliani, the prosecuting federal attorney on the case (who later became mayor of New York City), made the following statement: "On 106 occasions, bribes were offered or discussed.

On 105 of those occasions, the public official involved accepted the bribe. And on the other occasion, he turned it down because he didn't think the amount was large enough." [45]

Our influence on others will always be a reflection of what we are, not what we say. People become what we are, not what we say. We teach what we know and reproduce what we are. Integrity is always an inside job.

TRUSTWORTHINESS

A wise leader must be trustworthy:

At the end of the day, integrity is the big one. If people trust you, then you can get where you want to. But if people don't trust you, you have no chance. [46]
—Don Argus, managing director,
National Australia Bank

Trust is gained by being trustworthy with others' secrets. *"A talebearer reveals secrets, but he who is of a faithful spirit conceals a matter"* (Proverbs 11:13). This becomes the basis not only of a trusting relationship, but also of a compact bound together in love. *"He who covers a transgression seeks love, but he who repeats a matter separates friends"* (Proverbs 17:9).

We don't have to shout out our integrity if we're under attack. Truth always surfaces and is always vindicated. Or, to put it another way,

People of integrity expect to be believed. When they are not, they let time prove them right. [47]
—Scott Michael

Integrity is a victory, not a gift. There are moments every day of our lives when integrity will be under pressure.

We are regularly tempted to compromise an honest life. Integrity is not a given factor in everyone's life; rather, it is a result of self-discipline, inner trust, and the decision to be relentlessly honest.

To earn trust, a leader has to be authentic. People learn that what they hear, they understand, but what they see, they believe! What people need is a model to see, not a motto to say. Our tendency is to work harder on our images than on our integrity, but this is exactly the opposite of what it should be. Integrity comes first, and the image follows.

CHARACTER

Wise leaders are also individuals of upstanding character, for they realize that character is one of their greatest assets. As Billy Graham said,

When wealth is lost, nothing is lost; when health is lost, something is lost; when character is lost, all is lost. [48]

Essentially, character can be measured by what we do in private.

The measure of a man's real character is what he would do if he knew he would never be found out. [49]
—Thomas Babington, Lord Macauley

John Wooden, considered the greatest coach in the history of U.S. college basketball, was also an All-American as a basketball player at Purdue in 1930, 1931, and 1932. After becoming head coach at UCLA in 1948, his teams went on to set records for the longest winning streak and most championships (10) in NCAA history. One of the most powerful statements I've heard regarding character and leadership was from him. He said:

Ability may get you to the top, but it takes character to keep you there....Be more concerned with your character than with your reputation. Your character is what you really are while your reputation is merely what others think you are. [50]

In biblical terms, integrity is the "fear of God." This is important to note because, in many minds, integrity has simply become another route to success: "If I want to be successful, I'd better be true blue in my dealings with others." Whether it means we'll be successful or not, we must bind integrity to our whole way of life. In fact there will be times when honesty will seem to jeopardize success. Being committed to Christ means being committed to values no matter what the outcome.

The final estimate of men shows that history cares not an iota for the rank or title a man has borne, or the office he has held, but only the quality of his deeds and the character of his mind and heart. [51]
—Samuel Brengel,
Salvation Army evangelist

In other words, let the chips fall where they may, but we cannot afford to compromise truth in the inward parts as we attempt to gain success. We are called to hold to integrity in private, regardless of whether the end result is high success or deep failure. Our calling is to do right because we fear God. This awe of God, this love for Him, this jealousy for the honor of His name, and this high respect for His character will cause us to do the right thing for no other motive than our wish to please the Father and remain true to our commitment to Him.

When I began my Christian life, I had a job as a postman. At Christmas time we were all working much longer hours because of the greater volume of mail. From midday on, everyone was on overtime and, some days, triple pay. Everyone in the office signed off at 5 p.m. regardless of what time they actually finished, taking as much advantage of the increased cash as they could. I would look down the long list of sign-off times, but no matter how hard I tried, I could not bring myself to put down a time that was false. So, I would sign off at 2 or 3 p.m. or whatever time I finished.

We cannot afford to compromise truth in the inward parts as we attempt to gain success.

The other guys didn't appreciate it at all. It made them look bad. The boss even called me into his office to try to get me to put down the same time as everyone else, but my convictions were that I couldn't do it, so they put me on the longest run in the office. I was still finishing around 3 p.m., and I simply kept putting in the time I actually finished work.

When the pay packets were handed out after the Christmas period, I asked the guy next to me how much he got paid. He told me, and then I checked my own packet. I had been paid exactly the same! *"Asking no questions for conscience' sake"* (1 Corinthians 10:25), I exclaimed, "Thank You, Lord!"

Little things like this are what God watches in our developing years. He sees clearly whether money, position, or reputation are more important to us than integrity. We will face this question again and again throughout our lives.

Great leaders are truly great because they have private righteousness that's consistent with their public lives. Conversely, many powerful, successful leaders have forfeited the honor of their roles simply because they compromised private integrity.

> LORD, who may abide in Your tabernacle? Who may dwell in Your holy hill? He who walks uprightly, and works righteousness, and speaks the truth in his heart; he who does not backbite with his tongue, nor does evil to his neighbor, nor does he take up a reproach against his friend; in whose eyes a vile person is despised, but he honors those who fear the LORD; he who swears to his own hurt and does not change; he who does not put out his money at usury, nor does he take a bribe against the innocent. He who does these things shall never be moved. (Psalm 15:1–5)

As this verse reminds us, the person who lives a life of integrity is able to dwell in the presence of the Lord, ascend the holy hill of God, and *"never be moved."* The person without interior boundaries, however, will eventually be doomed. It is impossible not to be found out, for sin always surfaces.

Repentance is the only way to deal with sin. When we come into the light with our failures, only then will we be in line for the mercy of God; concealing our wrongs and attempting to get away with evil, however, inevitably ends in ruin. *"He who covers his sins will not prosper, but whoever confesses and forsakes them will have mercy"* (Proverbs 28:13).

Psalm 24 also extols the virtues of integrity, promising the ability to stand in the presence of God and receive the blessing of heaven and righteousness from God. The psalmist's four qualities of integrity are clean hands, a pure heart, trust in none other than God Himself, and honest speech.

Integrity needs to be the earmark of every Christian—and especially every Christian leader. Being two-faced is not an option.

Abraham Lincoln, not known for his good looks, was often ridiculed about his appearance. His character also came under all kinds of criticism, including accusations of hypocrisy. His response: "If I were two-faced, would I be wearing this one?"

Integrity needs to be the earmark of every Christian. Being two-faced is not an option.

Charles Spurgeon was famous for training individuals for the ministry as well as for leading one of the greatest churches of his time. In his lectures, he often referred to the need for strength of character in any effective leadership for God:

We need indomitable perseverance, dogged resolution, and a combination of sacred obstinacy, self-denial, holy gentleness, and invincible courage....

A man's life is always more forcible than his speech; when men take stock of him they reckon his deeds as pounds and his words as pence....

When the Devil turned preacher in our Lord's day, the Master bade him hold his peace; He did not care for satanic praises. It is very ridiculous to hear good truth from a bad man; it is like flour in a coal sack. [52]

RESPONSIBILITY

Wise leaders must be responsible leaders.

> I believe that every right implies a responsibility; every opportunity, an obligation; every possession, a duty. [53]
> —John D. Rockefeller Jr.,
> American industrialist and philanthropist

We live in a day when truth is expendable if it threatens to compromise a desired result. Our generation has come to believe that values are relative. We hope to avoid responsibility for our actions by blaming others, thereby making ourselves the victims rather than accepting responsibility for behaving morally before God, self, and others. Our tendency today is to absolve individuals of moral responsibility and treat them as victims of social circumstance.

We imagine that absolutes are a thing of the past, belonging to a bygone era, yet we continue to plummet down an apparently unstoppable spiral of epidemic drug use, youth suicides, family breakdowns, and violent crimes. We are just now beginning to reap the harvest of the "If it feels good, do it" philosophy of life.

If we ever needed people who live the message rather than just preach it, it is now. Aspiring to leadership is a great thing, but check the price tag first. The discipline of living right before God in secret is the key to a success that is granted from heaven. Any other kind is short-lived. As Philip Baker wrote in his book, *Secrets of Super Achievers*, "Those who excel in life usually have a strong faith in God, commitment to family, and a sense of values that causes them to live by conviction rather than preference." [54]

Chuck Colson was the famous "hatchet man" in the Watergate affair involving President Nixon in Washington, D.C., in the 1970s. After being involved in a number of nefarious exercises, certainly immoral for a leader, he served a prison sentence for his crimes. Chuck became a Christian during that time and has since learned what it is to be a privately "true" person. At a recent prayer breakfast I attended, he stated, "Public virtue does not create private virtue, but private virtue creates public virtue." [55] How true this is. The leader must be transformed from the inside out, not the other way around.

If we ever needed people who live the message rather than just preach it, it is now.

COURAGE

The second of the leader's "big three" is courage. A leader must have courage to do what is right, no matter what the consequences. As. C. S. Lewis has noted, courage is so important that it affects all other virtues:

Courage is not simply one of the virtues but the form of every virtue at the testing point.

God told Joshua to *"be strong and of good courage"* (Joshua 1:6). We can see from this Scripture that the quality of courage differs from that of strength, for Joshua was told to possess both.

Specifically, courage in a leader is the nerve that inspires followers to give the extraordinary. Some outstanding examples include David laughing and running toward the towering Goliath, fearless with an unswerving confidence in the Almighty; Churchill on the rooftops of government buildings during the Nazi bombings of London; El Cid, the legendary Spanish warrior of the eleventh century, leading the charge against the Mongols and inspiring his army on to victory, although it was only his dead corpse propped up in the saddle. Even perceived courage has the ability to inspire.

Courage is that quality in a person that is reckless of life, defying of death, and uncaring of reputation, comfort, and privilege. It leads a man or woman to take action for what is right, no matter what the cost. People rally to this blood, sweat, and tears kind of leadership because it touches the spiritual and the noble call of life deep within our souls.

"Moral courage is inextricably linked with physical courage. Physical courage is a willingness to incur danger when necessary."[56] Only two of Napoleon's marshals were older than forty. The great conqueror believed that younger leaders would be more daring in battle. Older ones, he thought, would try to protect their successful careers from blemish by choosing the safer, less dangerous course of action. But only those who take risks will succeed:

> **You cannot attain great success without**
> **taking great risks.**
> **—Anonymous**

Bravery is the quality that takes risks that have been shaped in God. The safe route has never yielded great victories. Stepping out of the boat is what Jesus calls us to do. The same Peter who took that step was the same man who chastised thousands of devout Jews on the day of Pentecost, winning them to the very Christ they had crucified not many days before.

One of history's most courageous leaders, Winston Churchill, had some amazing insights on the subject:

> One ought never to turn one's back on a threatened danger and try to run away from it. If you do that, you will double the danger. But if you meet it promptly and without flinching, you reduce the danger by half. Never run away from anything. Never! [57]

> Success is not final, failure is not fatal: it is the courage to continue that counts. [58]

> Courage is rightly esteemed the first of human qualities...because it is the quality which guarantees all others. [59]

Courage leads men and women to take action for what is right, no matter what the cost.

Courage grows and is contagious. David's confidence was so secure that he convinced Saul, the king of Israel and the tallest man in the nation, that he could kill the giant Goliath. This was a feat in itself. If Israel lost the contest, Saul would lose his throne and, at best, likely be dragged off to prison, or, at worst, be killed. The entire nation would become slaves to the Philistines, so it was a pretty big deal when King Saul rested the destiny of the entire nation upon the shoulders of young David, especially since David neither looked like a soldier nor was clothed as one. It was courage alone that clothed him.

Facing Goliath was not David's first encounter with danger. Even though he had only been a shepherd, he had rescued lambs from both lions and bears, killing the wild animals in the sheep's defense. His courage had grown with experience. We may feel as if the problems we face are larger than what we deserve, given our current level of responsibility, yet we are in a training program, readying for the days ahead when we will meet our Goliaths.

These moments of destiny will shape our leadership in life. If we fail to tackle what we face today, we will be ill equipped for what is coming tomorrow. Developing our leadership potential is not just about acquiring skills but more so about building courage to face ever bigger giants.

Courage is the quality that takes risks for what has to be done in order to complete the job. Courage is doing what must be done in spite of fears that rage in the soul. Courage is refusing to cave in to fears when they make their presence known. Courage is facing an impossible task, experiencing fear, and yet doing it anyway. Courage is the defining difference between those who achieve greatness and those who do not.

Courage is fear turned inside out. It is impossible to be courageous if at first you weren't afraid. [60]
— Dr. Bob Rotella, sports psychologist

The leader who refuses to move until fear has gone will never move. He or she must show courage in the midst of that fear instead.

Abraham was definitely one of the greatest figures of leadership in the history of the world, even though his influence began late in life. He stepped out of the known into the unknown at age seventy-five. God told him to leave his family, his home, his country, and to go to a land that God would show him. Abraham obeyed and was so sure of his mission that he convinced hundreds of others to go with him from Haran. They too left the known "home turf" to go to this place that God was going to show him. Influence comes when we step out with a vision of the invisible.

Andy Stanley, pastor of the great North Point Community Church in Atlanta, Georgia, wrote this about the necessity of courage in the life of a leader:

> Courage is essential to leadership because the first person who steps out in a new direction is viewed as the leader. And being the first to step out requires courage. In this way, *courage establishes leadership*.... Leaders provide a mental picture of a preferred future and then ask people to follow them there. Leaders require those around them to abandon the known and embrace the unknown—with no guarantee of success. As leaders, we are asking men and women not only to follow us to a place *they* have never been before; we are asking them to follow us to a place *we* have never been before either....Leadership takes the courage to walk in the dark. The darkness is the uncertainty that always accompanies change. [61]

How do we "learn" courage? Let me share a great story I read on how to do this:

> "So, you think I'm courageous?" the woman asked.

> "Yes, I do."

> "Perhaps I am. But that's because I've had some inspiring teachers. I'll tell you about one of them. Many years ago, when I worked as a volunteer at Stanford Hospital,

I got to know a little girl named Liza who was suffering from a rare and serious disease. Her only chance of recovery appeared to be a blood transfusion from her five-year-old brother, who had miraculously survived the same disease and had developed the antibodies needed to combat the illness. The doctor explained the situation to her little brother and asked the boy if he would be willing to give his blood to his sister. I saw him hesitate for only a moment before taking a deep breath and saying, 'Yes, I'll do it if it will save Liza.'

"As the transfusion progressed, he lay in bed next to his sister and smiled, as we all did, seeing the color returning to her cheeks. Then his face grew pale and his smile faded. He looked up at the doctor and asked with a trembling voice, 'Will I start to die right away?'

"Being young, the boy had misunderstood the doctor; he thought he was going to have to give her all his blood.

"Yes, I've learned courage," she added, "because I've had inspiring teachers." [62]

Courage is the defining difference between those who achieve greatness and those who do not.

Courage is something we must choose to do. And the benefits are great. Unsolved problems are gateways to the future, but only courageous people will tackle them.

In short, courage is taking a stand when no one else will. It is standing for something that is right even though it is unpopular. Great leaders are not fearful of the opinions of others. They live in the wisdom that fears God more. They are committed to the right no matter what the cost. This courage wins the hearts of everybody. And this is where leaders show their calling.

> How far would Moses have gone if he had taken a poll in Egypt? What would Jesus Christ have preached if he had taken a poll in the land of Israel? What would have happened to the Reformation if Martin Luther had taken a poll? It isn't polls or public opinion of the moment that counts. It's right and wrong and leadership. [63]
> —Harry S. Truman, 33rd President of the United States

STRENGTH

The third quality of the leader's "big three" is strength. Leaders must have strength to continue through to the end, to stick to what they've begun.

The apostle Paul prayed for the Ephesians—and for *"the whole family in heaven and earth,"* which includes us—that the Holy Spirit would impart to us mighty strength *"in the inner man."*

> *For this reason I bow my knees to the Father of our Lord Jesus Christ, from whom the whole family in heaven and earth is named, that He would grant you, according to the riches of His glory, to be strengthened with might through His Spirit in the inner man.*
> (Ephesians 3:14–16)

Ed Cole, calling for a revival of manhood, wrote, "In these tough times, the world is crying out for strong men.

It needs men who can overcome drifting philosophies and restore order, hope, dignity, and heroic action." [64]

Throughout Scripture, God calls for strength in His servants so that the work of the kingdom can be done. If leaders are strong, then their teams will be strong as well. And if the team is strong, then the people they lead will be strong.

> *"Yet now be strong, Zerubbabel," says the LORD; "and be strong, Joshua, son of Jehozadak, the high priest; and be strong, all you people of the land," says the LORD, "and work; for I am with you," says the LORD of hosts.*
> (Haggai 2:4)

Strength is a powerful factor in the growth of an organization. The level of strength in leadership determines the maximum limit of the organization, be it a church, a small business, a ministry, or a corporation.

Strength is a powerful factor in the growth of an organization.

The pressures are many. It takes strong people to handle the varied stresses. Once leaders have reached their limits, unless they grow personally, their organizations will cease to grow and will remain in a more manageable state for the leader.

We know we are reaching our limits when...

❖ Our conversations center around how exhausted we are.

❖ Our view of the organization sounds negative.

❖ We notice the intrusion of people too much: "The phone never stops ringing."

❖ We habitually complain about our remuneration: "It's not enough; it's never enough."

❖ We're always attempting to "get away."

These things can be valid problems. If they are, then we should fix them. If we are focused on these things, however, then our lives will not be happy. We simply will not grow.

WE RISE TO THE LEVEL OF OUR LOWEST CEILING

The purpose of God demands that we remain strong—physically, emotionally, mentally, and spiritually. A commonly accepted observation called the Peter Principle is defined by *Merriam-Webster's Collegiate Dictionary, Eleventh Edition* as the theory that an employee within an organization will advance to his or her level of incompetence and then remain there—hence, the need to grow beyond our limitations. Every leader needs to rise to higher levels to fulfill his or her calling.

Again and again, Joshua was instructed to be strong as he assumed the mantle of leadership over Israel:

❖ Moses told him to *"be strong"* (Deuteronomy 31:23) when he commissioned Joshua.

❖ God told him three times to *"be strong"* (Joshua 1:6, 7, 9).

❖ The Israelites told him to *"be strong"* (Joshua 1:18).

Strength comes from God Himself. Even Jesus, as He agonized and surrendered in prayer before the crucifixion, was strengthened by an angel sent from heaven so that He could carry out the will of the Father (Luke 22:43). This is where strength lies—in God, in His Word, and in His Spirit.

But those who wait on the LORD shall renew their strength; they shall mount up with wings like eagles, they shall run and not be weary, they shall walk and not faint. (Isaiah 40:31)

When we compromise our devotion to the Lord through the seduction of the world, we dilute our strength, following Samson's sorry example.

Every leader needs to rise to higher levels to fulfill his or her calling.

The strength of the leader governs his or her level of achievement. In other words, we rise to the level of our lowest ceiling. No matter how talented or educated we may be, or how fortunate our circumstances are, when we reach the upper limit of our capacities, we can go no farther.

THE SPIRITUAL CEILING

If our spiritual lives are not equal to the amount of work and responsibility we have, sooner or later our attitudes will sour, and we will be overcome. When the conditioning influence of prayer and the Word is not happening, the power to forgive those who offend is absent, and so people will be scattered. The power to resist temptation and compromise is weakened. The ability to believe and stay in faith under pressure is disarmed. Our fight against Satan is diluted. Our perspective is distorted as we view things naturally instead of from a heavenly perspective. All these factors limit growth as the ceiling is reached again.

This is why, when it comes to church leadership, revival is so essential to the life of the church and the pastor. I make sure we have a series of revival meetings at least twice a year in our church so that our people and our leaders, including myself, are all revived with fresh, supernatural encounters with God. We cannot afford to let the fire go out. Everything we do for God in the church depends on the level of fire burning within us for God and His purpose. This needs regular refueling in all of us.

There are a lot of things called revival today, but it seems that few ever actually achieve that purpose. Revival is not revival if people don't recover or increase their prayer life, their consecration to God, their service to the Lord, or if they don't reach out to the unchurched. If meetings stir up a lot of emotion and phenomena but people are basically the same afterward, then these meetings cannot be called revivals. They might be called "healing services" or "evangelism crusades." However, real revival stirs the flames of believers to fresh devotion to Christ.

The strength of the leader governs his or her level of achievement.

In particular, the leader needs regular reviving. Discouragement threatens the leader's enthusiasm constantly. The difficult problems, the weight of the call, the responsibilities—all can deplete the spiritual life of a church leader. Time away for rest is important. Even more important, though, is time given to personal spiritual revival.

THE PHYSICAL CEILING

We may be spiritually, emotionally, and mentally strong, but if our physical stamina cannot cope with a heavy schedule, we become exhausted and unable to continue in our leadership role.

Consider Evan Roberts, a key figure in the Welsh revival. He lasted two years before he had a physical breakdown. Charles Finney, who spearheaded the Second Great Awakening revival meetings for about ten years, during which time some 500,000 people came to Christ, took only about seven days rest in that entire time. After the ten years, he grew ill and was limited to teaching in a Bible school for half the year and evangelizing the other half. He wrote, "My health soon became such that I found I must relinquish one of my fields of endeavor." [65]

How much more could these people have done if they had been physically well, through proper care of their physical bodies as temples of the Holy Spirit? The macho mentality that says things like "I never take a break," or "We haven't had a vacation in years," fails to impress. We're behaving no better than egotistical rebels with statements like these. Even God rested after a week's work. Who do we think we are?

Being a leader is physically demanding work. A leader needs to be healthy and strong. This means that sound sleep, good eating habits, and fitness all need to be incorporated into the daily routine. It is not right to dismiss these things as unimportant and believe everything will be all right. If I am tired, I am less effective in every area. Whatever spiritual gifts we have will not function with the same level of fruitfulness if we do not take care of our physical bodies.

We need to go to bed early enough to rise and begin the day with prayer. We need to take enough time off on a regular basis before we desperately need to get away from it all. Some illnesses are simply normal physiological reactions taking place because the body is tired and the defense systems are weak. If we won't stop to rest of our own volition, sickness will stop us instead. We need to eliminate junk foods that are loaded with sugars and fats because we will become worn out trying to digest it all. We need to take time each day to exercise as well. Jogging, swimming, or some other sport keeps us fit and helps us to stay strong.

A sound heart is life to the body.   (Proverbs 14:30)

THE EMOTIONAL CEILING

Our emotional ceilings prevent some of us from delegating responsibilities. We become too anxious to let go of areas that are critical to the life of our organization. Sometimes we feel that delegation involves too much trust and produces too much anxiety. However, increasing our faith, training others, and requiring higher levels of accountability raise our ceilings in this area.

Hurts, offenses, and demands should not overwhelm us with hatred and anger. Attitudes must be kept healthy by regularly forgiving those who have wronged us. Losing our tempers, nursing anger, and giving up on people are all signs of emotional burnout. If we cry easily over things that normally wouldn't upset us, then we are hitting our emotional ceiling.

We increase the strength of our emotional capabilities by taking rest. In the realm of church leadership, many ministers relate to "Monday-itis" when low feelings seem to discolor all the positives of the Sunday just past. This is simply an emotional low. The tank needs to be refilled. This is easily accomplished by simply spending time in quiet and letting ourselves revive. When we're emotionally drained, depression and anger come easily. After a few hours of uninterrupted quietness, however, emotions are amazingly renewed.

Our emotional ceilings prevent some of us from delegating responsibilities.

Rest doesn't come from endless entertainment, noise, and activity. There simply have to be times when we get away from all the activity. Jesus told His disciples, *"'Come* [apart] *by yourselves to a deserted place and rest a while.' For there were many coming and going, and they did not even have time to eat"* (Mark 6:31). A friend of mine adds, "before you come apart."

THE MENTAL CEILING

Mental strength is extremely important. We must be able to put troublesome people out of our minds. They should not be able to distract our focus. This relates to casting our cares on the Lord (1 Peter 5:7). When we're weak, our minds default to anxiety. It takes enormous mental strength to cast worries from our thinking and forget them.

Most of us remember the things we should forget and forget the things we should remember. A weak mind will continue to wrestle with past crises and concerns. Such a mind will become fixed on the negatives, the consequence of which is living with black, cloudy thoughts. A weak mind is unable to concentrate under pressure. Tasks are completed with great difficulty when pressure mounts. Listening to people's problems becomes almost impossible.

Even though we may be extremely talented in some areas of our lives, even though we may have wide and extraordinary experiences, if our minds cannot cope with making bold decisions, we will rise not to the level of our talents and gifts, but only to the level of our mental strength. Even if we do manage to exceed the ceiling briefly, our weak area will bring us back to the level of manageability.

This is why it is imperative to engage in initiating growth in our lives consistently—adding qualities of character to our makeup and learning new and better skills for living. As we develop friendships with people who have progressed further than we have, we learn how to live in dimensions we've not entered before.

THE SOCIAL CEILING

The leader must have good social strengths. If the opinions of others matter too much to us, our relationships with God, others, and ourselves will be weak. We must be able to say no to requests even though they are genuine. We need to be able to shift gears in relationships.

When we delegate responsibilities, we develop new relationships and sever old ones. This can easily cause resentment and present challenges to old friends and acquaintances. If we are overly sensitive to this, we will weaken and not go through with the brief, emotionally difficult time of change.

It is inevitable that we will have to confront people over issues throughout our time in leadership. Sometimes they will be people who are close to us. We must be strong enough to deal with these situations. They will not get better by themselves. Talking to someone about areas or issues that must be challenged is a very demanding task. However, once a problem is lanced, everyone feels better, and the sore spot can heal.

Many of us remember the things we should forget and forget the things we should remember.

It is a good idea to have predetermined standard policies that relate to general situations rather than having to deal with individuals on a case-by-case basis. Applying a preset policy can remove pressure from your personal relationship with a person. For example, sometimes friends ask if I could arrange for them to preach in churches, usually overseas, where I have existing relationships. I have found this places stress on my relationship with these churches. The church may not want to turn me down, but they are also unsure about whether they want an unknown person preaching in their church. Thus, I have a standing policy that I do not arrange speaking engagements for others. I will offer to write a letter of introduction, but that's all. Once they have met the local pastor, he can make up his mind as to whether he wants to allow the visitor to preach or not.

These kinds of policies help you explain to friends and others that this is how you operate. Preset policies remove offense from an event and keep a relationship intact.

In Exodus 18:21, Moses had to identify individuals who could lead groups of ten, fifty, a hundred, or thousands, and appoint them accordingly. The mistake we sometimes make is to position someone with exceptional talent in an area of oversight, thinking that he or she will be able to lead people. This is often not the case, especially with artistic people. Often the sheer weight of responsibility crushes their capacity to lead or even manage. It is frequently better to place an obvious leader over an area rather than a person who has the talent or skills for that area but who is not a leader.

GROWING BEYOND OUR CEILINGS

As leaders, we continually need to grow personally so that we increase our capacity for greater accomplishments. We learn from everyone we meet. We fellowship so that we mix with people who stretch us. We grow through trials. We grow as we step out in faith. We grow as we accept more challenging levels of responsibility. As leaders, we need to continue to attempt greater and greater things because we know this is key to growth. We must refuse to remain in a zone where we are not stretched.

Our ceilings rise higher as our abilities to handle greater challenges increase. The ceilings we reach are not intended to limit us; they simply indicate where our capacity level is at the current time. They reveal areas in which we need to grow.

The ceilings we reach are not intended to limit us; they simply indicate where our capacity level is.

What worried us yesterday can't touch us today. We laugh about things that would have crippled us years ago. The things that worry us today, that we complain about today, that we are discouraged about today, we will laugh about tomorrow as we grow and become the bigger people

God destines us to be. The amounts and numbers we're dealing with today will seem tiny as we grow with God into His enormously wonderful plan for our lives.

> *Till we all come...to the measure of the stature of the fullness of Christ.* (Ephesians 4:13)

eleven

****

THE LEADER IS
A PEOPLE PERSON

****

Only basic goodness gives life to technique.
—Steven Covey

Today's great leaders have great people skills. They excel in relating to other people, whether the relationship is minor and brief or deep and lifelong. Without a doubt, I have no hesitation in saying that the highest proportion of our success in accomplishing God's purpose depends on the success of our relationships. Great leaders understand that their authority is not based on their titles, their positions, or their seniority, but on their relationships with the people they lead. Followers must feel they are people, not just numbers, statistics, resources, or the means to achieving the goals of the organization.

The essence of any great relationship is love. This does not mean that the leader must always encompass the highest expressions of love. At its simplest level, to love people is to enjoy them. This means I enjoy people when I meet them. This doesn't come naturally or even easily to task-oriented personalities, but love is as much a decision as a spontaneous feeling. Loving people is often learned. There are few people we meet whom we find ourselves loving without any effort. Loving people means treating them well, making sacrifices for their benefit, and helping them to achieve their needs and their dreams.

Followers must feel they are people, not just numbers, statistics, or resources.

The secret of great writers lies not just in their literary skills; the secret is their love for people, their fascination with others. This surfaces in their writing. The secret of great pastors is that they love their people. The secret of great employers, military commanders, or leaders of any kind is love for those they are leading or influencing. Surveys reveal that people's greatest sense of need is not money or health, but communication and loving relationships.[66] No one seems to feel confident about their roles, feelings, and expectations in relationships—or even about how to relate to others, no matter what the level of closeness may be.

Consistently at the top of needs charts is not, as many might expect, success, youth, good looks, or any of those enviable assets. The clear winner is relationships, close ones, followed by happy marriages. "Supportive, intimate connections with other people seem tremendously important," says psychologist David Myers. "The least happy people are those in unhappy marriages. Happiest are those who are married to their 'best friend.'" [67]

Throughout the twentieth century and into the twenty-first, the family has suffered an onslaught that has brought about an amazing breakdown of communications within the home. "Technology has given us the dishwasher, the micro-wave oven, and the VCR. All have served to dislocate and fragment the family. Family members can now eat, clean up, and watch television separately and selectively." [68]

We have imagined that family ties are deep enough to keep us all together. We pray that high values in our life-style will keep us in some kind of harmony with others. We think that being romantically "in love" will be enough for a marriage to survive. We hope friendship will empower us through the difficulties we face. However, this view has been proven to be naïve and misguided. Relationships don't just happen; they take work.

GETTING TO WORK

Certain skills are essential to successful relationships. We ignore these at our own peril. Some of them are so simple that they escape us, and some are so obvious we're embarrassed to use them. Great relational skills are like everything else; given attention, they become good habits in our lives.

What are these amazing relational skills? They are not techniques for gaining advantage over others. They are not heartless, insincere gimmicks for selling goods or promoting products. If we fail to possess genuine interest in people, no matter how many relational skills we might possess, we will ring like a hollow gong in their ears. Living successfully with other people always begins and ends with love. Steven Covey has put it as well as anyone I know: "Only basic goodness gives life to technique." [69]

Living successfully with other people always begins and ends with love.

God's love has been *"poured out in our hearts by the Holy Spirit"* (Romans 5:5). As we *"put on love"* (Colossians 3:14) and begin to enact love toward others, that great love of God rises in us, and we are found to be representing God's kind of leadership to those around us.

The Bible contains many key principles that help us relate successfully to others. Here are a few:

MAKE EVERYONE YOUR TEACHER

> *Give instruction to a wise man, and he will be still wiser; teach a just man, and he will increase in learning.* (Proverbs 9:9)

The famous nineteenth century American essayist and poet, Ralph Waldo Emerson, who is considered the first distinctively American author to influence European thought, said, "Every man is my superior in some way; in that, I can learn from him." [70]

Every person knows something more than we do in some area. Ask people about their areas of expertise. Learn something. If we think we know everything, our conceit will not be hidden. People will roll their eyes when we talk. We shouldn't be self-congratulatory. If we are to be praised, it should come from the mouths of others, never our own (Proverbs 27:2). It is a relief to find someone who values and esteems others enough to be genuinely interested in their lives.

All people have a deep craving to know that they make a difference in the world, to know they're somehow significant, that their lives mean something. The startling thing about this is that you and I have the power to satisfy that craving. We are able to make everyone we meet realize their significance by learning from them.

I have learned this from some of the greatest people I know. When I was just a hopeful young preacher, I was invited to speak in some afternoon electives at a minister's conference. To my amazement, a large crowd gathered in the room. On the front row was Trevor Chandler, a legend of faith in our part of the world. As I was speaking, he was taking notes. I couldn't believe it. He was over three times my age and still he was taking notes on what I was speaking. This had a major impact on me. I was humbled and inspired at the same time by the man's humility and hunger.

Another time, Dr. Robert Schuller was preaching in our church. Out in the back room before the service, he asked me what I thought about particular things that were happening in the church around the world. I was still only a young pastor at the time, yet this world-renowned figure was asking for my opinion.

All of us have the chance to make someone else realize his or her significance every day. Let others be your teacher.

BECOME HUMBLE

Humility is something we do to ourselves (James 4:10). We must be secure in ourselves. Even though He is God, Jesus voluntarily took on the form of a servant, made Himself of zero reputation, obeyed commands, and died the death of a common criminal in order to serve the needs of others.

When He was about to die, He washed His disciples' feet. He was able to do these humbling things because He knew where He had come from, where He was going, and that all things were placed in His hands (John 13:3). From this position of security, He could humble Himself without fear.

All people have a deep craving to know that they make a difference in the world.

When we provide a secure environment of acceptance, people can become unassuming more easily than if we are attempting to put them in their place. This involves valuing others more highly than we do ourselves.

Let nothing be done through selfish ambition or conceit, but in lowliness of mind let each esteem others better than himself. (Philippians 2:3)

Find a person's point of honor and give it to them. Show respect for an individual's title, name, heritage, experience, and position in life. Respect for others reveals that we are secure. We don't have to bring people down a peg or two.

We're quite happy to give honor where honor is due (Romans 13:7).

LISTEN AND LET OTHERS DO THE TALKING

**The reason we have two ears and only one mouth
is that we may listen more and talk less.
—Zeno of Citium, early Greek philosopher
and founder of Stoicism**

In the multitude of words sin is not lacking, but he who restrains his lips is wise. (Proverbs 10:19)

So then, my beloved brethren, let every man be swift to hear, slow to speak, slow to wrath. (James 1:19)

Do you see a man hasty in his words? There is more hope for a fool than for him. (Proverbs 29:20)

In short, listen to people when they are talking. Charles W. Elliot, the former president of Harvard University, had keen insight into the importance of listening. He said,

**There is no mystery about successful business....
Exclusive attention to the person speaking
is very important. Nothing else is
so flattering as that.** [71]

To build on this, nothing is ruder than not listening.

Children know they are loved when their parents stop whatever they are doing and listen to them. We must convey the same love and interest in those we lead.

Dale Carnegie, in his book *How to Win Friends and Influence People*, relates this story:

One morning years ago, an angry customer stormed into the office of Julian F. Detmer, founder of the Detmer Woolen Company, which later became the world's largest distributor of woolens to the tailoring trade.

"This man owed us a small sum of money," Mr. Detmer explained to me. "The customer denied it, but we knew he was wrong. So our credit department had insisted that he pay. After getting a number of letters from our credit department, he packed his grip, made a trip to Chicago, and hurried into my office to inform me not only that he was not going to pay that bill, but that he was never going to buy another dollar's worth of goods from the Detmer Woolen Company.

"I listened patiently to all he had to say. I was tempted to interrupt, but I realized that would be bad policy, so I let him talk himself out. When he finally simmered down and got in a receptive mood, I said quietly: 'I want to thank you for coming to Chicago to tell me about this. You have done me a great favor, for if our credit department has annoyed you, it may annoy other good customers, and that would be just too bad. Believe me, I am far more eager to hear this than you are to tell it.'

"That was the last thing in the world he expected me to say. I think he was a trifle disappointed, because he had come to Chicago to tell me a thing or two, but here I was thanking him instead of scrapping with him. I assured him we would wipe the charge off the books and forget it, because he was a very careful man with only one account to look after, while our clerks had to look after thousands. Therefore, he was less likely to be wrong than we were.

"I told him that I understood exactly how he felt and that, if I were in his shoes, I should undoubtedly feel precisely as he did. Since he wasn't going to buy from us anymore, I recommended some other woolen houses.

"In the past, we had usually lunched together when he came to Chicago, so I invited him to have lunch with me this day. He accepted reluctantly, but when we came back to the office he placed a larger order than ever before. He returned home in a softened mood and, wanting to be just as fair with us as we had been with him, looked over his bills, found one that had been mislaid, and sent us a check with his apologies.

"Later, when his wife presented him with a baby boy, he gave his son the middle name of Detmer, and he remained a friend and customer of the house until his death twenty-two years afterwards." [72]

It is said that if an organization listens to the complaint of a customer and the problem is fixed, the customer remains a loyal customer and tells approximately seven others about the experience. Conversely, if a person is ignored and the problem not fixed, that customer will not deal with that organization anymore and will tell approximately twenty other people about the negative experience.

COMMUNICATE WITH RESPECT

If we don't know much about the topic of conversation, we reveal our ignorance by wading in where angels fear to tread: *"Even a fool is counted wise when he holds his peace; when he shuts his lips, he is considered perceptive"* (Proverbs 17:28).

If you want people to avoid you, laugh at you behind your back, and despise you, here is the recipe:

❖ Never listen to anyone for very long.

❖ Talk incessantly about yourself.

❖ If you have an idea while another person is talking, interrupt.

❖ Concentrate on what you want to say next, and make your statement.

❖ Look away from the person who is speaking. Strike up a conversation with someone else.

We must indicate to the person we are talking with that he or she is the most important person to us right then.

"He who answers a matter before he hears it, it is folly and shame to him" (Proverbs 18:13). For this reason, turn cell phones off at lunch. Turn the television off. Don't answer the phone during dinner. These actions all indicate to the person we are talking with that he or she is the most important person to us right then.

Some basics regarding communication and relating to others are:

❖ Use "us" and "we" instead of "you," "they," and "them." Instead of "You need to become far more enthusiastic," say "We need to...."

❖ Use "and'" instead of "but." "Yes, but don't you know..." versus "Yes, and do you know also...." Talk in terms of agreement, not disagreement. Many people need a "but-ectomy." Change your "but" to "and."

❖ Begin conversations with questions: "What?" "Who?" "Which?" "When?" and "How?" but not "Why?" It implies suspicion.

❖ Tell people that they are already what you are expecting them to be. It's not "You need to be unique," but, "You are unique."

❖ Don't tell people that you believe they can do it. If you believe that they can achieve something, then just tell them directly. The fact that you believe in them is inherent in your statement. It's not, "I believe you can do it," but, "You can do it, of course you can."

❖ Make sure that your conversations are dialogues, not monologues. If people don't reply at appropriate moments when we are talking, then something is wrong in the conversation. If we have a lecturing tone in our voice, people become quiet and won't reply, except in hostility. A conversation is two or more people talking with each other, not just one person talking at the others.

❖ Speak in short, relevant sentences. Keep everyone involved in the conversation. If we take too long to say our piece, people lose the rhythm of the conversation— they then seek to simply end it and get away.

❖ Make sure other people talk. Once they are talking, don't interrupt them. When others begin talking in the natural rhythm of the conversation, hold your thought and invite their comments. When they've finished, don't raise your voice and speak faster to keep them from starting again.

Dr. Gerald Nirenberg says, "Cooperativeness in conversation is achieved when you show that you consider the other person's ideas and feelings as important as your own.... Accepting his or her viewpoint will encourage the listener to have an open mind toward your ideas." [73]

Show Interest in People

People are fascinating. Ask about their work. Be positive about what they do, no matter what it is. There's always something positive in what others do. It is easy to be fascinated by someone famous or entranced by the stories of some great adventurer, but few people have these kinds of life experiences. Most are living what they imagine to be pretty ordinary lives.

We can be artists with people's lives. As we show our excitement about what they do, their lives are valued.

Marshall McLuhan, the great twentieth-century media philosopher, is attributed as having said, "Art is making the ordinary extraordinary." He was referring to those artists who take things like a kitchen tap and bolt it to the wall in an art gallery. Initially, many have been quite critical of these forms of modern art, wondering where the artistic value is. However, the housewife's world has been suddenly enhanced; the things she deals with every day have been transformed into pieces of art! They have new value and interest.

We can be artists with people's lives. We find the value in what they do, whether they are wealthy, aged investors or poor, young apprentices. Whether they are homemakers or demolition experts, people are fascinating. As we show our excitement about what they do, their lives are valued.

Some people who work hard feel their achievements are insignificant, especially in comparison to what others are doing. Those who have achieved great heights intimidate most of us. That is why we must encourage everyone, especially when it comes to doing things for the Lord. We should encourage anyone who is doing good in this life. We must let them know that what they are doing has eternal consequences. Be enthusiastic about all the achievements, big or small, in the lives of others; appearances can be deceiving.

When people lose weight or kick a bad habit, congratulate them and ask them how they did it. Tell them you realize how hard it is to achieve these kinds of things. When people have new clothes, a new car, a new house or job, congratulate them and tell them that they deserve it. Be interested in where they got it and how it's working. It amazes me how many people are negative about their own lives. All it takes is someone telling them how positive their lives are for them to change that view.

REMEMBER NAMES

Everyone's name is important to the individual. Remembering people's names communicates our interest in them. There are a number of methods designed to help us remember names. It is said that Charles Schwab, the first man in America to be paid one million dollars a year, could remember the names of 50,000 people. I've gasped when I've heard of ministers who know the names of most of the people in their churches, especially when the congregation exceeds a thousand people.

I find that if I introduce myself with my own name, this prompts people to reply with theirs. I also repeat the name several times in the conversation immediately after I have been introduced. Find whatever technique works for you to program names into your memory bank—the dividends will multiply.

Introduce People to Others

Introduce new acquaintances to your circle of friends and contacts. No matter how brief the conversation may have been, it is memorable in the minds of those for whom you arranged the contact. Networking is one of the most powerful ways we can assist others. We shouldn't "hog" relationships for ourselves. We will always benefit more by including people rather than excluding them. People have their horizons expanded by meeting others who have traveled further.

Make Everyone You Meet Feel Significant

Remind people of their accomplishments. Appreciate any impact they have made in your life, and thank them specifically for what they have meant to you. A sense of destiny lies within every soul. A sense of significance is vital to the health of each person. Love is the quality that supplies this need.

Just saying that it is love, however, is too vague. Love manifests in many distinct ways. In this context, it is a matter of congratulating people on their successes. This runs against the grain in many people's minds because there is a tendency to be suspicious of anyone else's success. Far too often, jealousy robs us of the joy of other people's blessings.

It has been said that only half the people who are institutionalized for mental illness can have their problem accounted for by biological causes. Others have simply slipped into a delusional state; often they imagine being some great figure in history or they are living out the life of a person they greatly admire. The need we all have for significance is enormous. The wonderful thing is that we have it in our power to grant that significance to others by recognizing even the smallest blessing they have been to others or ourselves.

VALUE PEOPLE

When I was a child, my mother told me not to run out on the road when my ball bounced into the traffic. Her warning was, "We can always get another ball, but we can't get another you." I've never forgotten that. Little phrases like that in the minds of children—or adults, for that matter— help us realize we are valuable in this life. Someone else wants us around.

Remind people of their accomplishments. Thank them specifically for what they have meant to you.

When I was just a young youth leader in a church, a pastor by the name of Peter Garret asked me to preach at his church family camp. This was a great honor because I was just a youth leader. Here I was teaching the adults, grownups! It was a wonderful privilege. At the end of the camp, he handed me an honorarium of about $600. This was in 1972. I was just a young preacher who had hardly ever received any kind of love offering for preaching anywhere. My feelings of worth went through the roof! They didn't have to give me a penny. I was having enough fun just preaching. But they did. That $600 meant far more to me than just the cash value. It was a major moment of encouragement in my life.

We show true appreciation with more than just our words. The words need to have something of substance attached—some personal investment or effort. Otherwise, they can be interpreted as cheap and meaningless.

BE EXTRAVAGANT IN YOUR PRAISE

If we tell a person that he or she is "somewhat interesting" or "doing all right," it is more like a slap in the face than a compliment. The very nature of praise is that it ignores faults and amplifies good points. Praise often needs to be overstated in order for it to cut through all the negatives and reach the person's heart.

Whenever you have the opportunity to speak in a public setting, no matter how small, mention other people by name, and call attention to their achievements.

If we tell a person he or she is "somewhat interesting," it is more like a slap in the face than a compliment.

Praise a mother's children. Tell her positive things about her children, such as that they're well dressed, well behaved, and looking healthy. A mother's life is invested in her children. If they are failing, she feels it reflects on her.

There is always something positive about every child. Find it. You may have to think hard, dig deep, and search.

However, a rebellious kid can be "independent," a noisy kid can be "spirited."

As a side note, children generally like to be thought of as being older than they are. Geoff Fenholt, who played the part of Jesus in *Jesus Christ Superstar* on Broadway, sang in our church one Sunday. Afterward, lots of young people crowded around him, and he guessed the ages of several. He was off by two or three years, always older than their actual ages. I told him he must be aging because he thought all these kids were two years older than they really were. He said, "No, I do it on purpose. You watch them straighten up and feel good when you think they're that grown up." As a caution, never try this with anyone above the age of 25; what was a compliment in younger years soon becomes derisive. If anything, subtract several years instead of adding them.

Congratulate people's successes. Praise their work. Find significant points of their occupation, and praise them for what they do.

Praise a child's mother and father. Or praise grandchildren to their grandparents and watch them beam. *"Children's children are the crown of old men, and the glory of children is their father"* (Proverbs 17:6).

Never criticize parents to their children, even if they are critical of their parents.

Respect older people and show them honor. Express it directly to them.

Respect Everyone

Give due respect to all who have titles or honor of any kind. (Romans 13:7). Address people by their titles unless you have been invited to be on a first-name basis. Don't attempt to equalize everybody; this reveals your insecurities and meanness of spirit. Be generous in your praise and admiration of others. Respect those opposed to you, and you will win their favor.

Abraham Lincoln was clearly one of the greatest leaders in history, galvanizing the United States to come together when the nation was under enormous threat of division, emancipating the slaves of the South, and securing victory in a terrible civil war. By the time Lincoln took office, seven states had seceded from the Union. Ten days before Lincoln took the oath of office on March 4, 1861, Jefferson Davis was sworn in as president of the Confederacy. President Buchanan had already given up hope of holding the country together and was simply waiting for his term to expire. Moreover, Buchanan left Washington, D.C., proclaiming that he was "the last President of the United States."

Give due respect to all who have titles or honor of any kind.

In addition, the United States Congress had not taken any action whatsoever to put down the rebellion. While a bill was tabled in the House of Representatives that gave the President power to call out the state militia, the Senate passed a resolution requesting the war department to lower military spending. All this happened between the time Lincoln was elected and the time he took office. Lincoln was faced with the realization that the South had taken control of all federal agencies and had seized almost every fort and arsenal in Southern territory. Washington, D.C., was left almost completely defenseless, protected only by a portion of the nation's army, which in 1861 was unprepared for war. The U.S. Army was a scattered, dilapidated, poorly equipped, and disorganized gang of some 16,000 soldiers, many of whom sympathized with the South.

Rumors persisted that Lincoln's inauguration was to be disrupted, the President killed, and the city taken by the Confederates. When Lincoln delivered his first Inaugural Address, the nation was in a crisis more severe and ominous than at any other time. The country was divided, hatred was the most prevalent emotion, and there was no effective leadership anywhere in the government. In the midst of all this turmoil, the relatively unknown Abraham Lincoln took the oath of office as the nation's sixteenth President. The first Republican President, elected by a minority of the popular vote, he was a Washington outsider who was widely viewed as a second-rate country lawyer, completely ill equipped and unable to handle the presidency.

Donald Philips, in his book *Lincoln on Leadership*, tells us that Abraham Lincoln listened, paid attention, and established trust. He worked hard at forging strong relationships with all of his subordinates, especially the members of his cabinet and his commanding generals. William H. Seward, Lincoln's Secretary of State, initially thought the President to be well intentioned yet totally unqualified to run the administration and lead the country. However, he found the President-elect to be firm and resourceful, with a distinct mind of his own. He became so frustrated in his efforts to change Lincoln's mind that he submitted his resignation even before the inauguration. Lincoln met with Seward and, by appealing to his patriotic duty and sense of self-worth, persuaded him to stay on.

The overzealous Secretary of State then sent the President a chastising memorandum, outlining what he felt the policy should be toward the South. Lincoln promptly responded with a letter of his own. "If such policies were to be instituted," wrote Lincoln, "I must do it."

Seward and Lincoln soon became allies. The President often stopped by the Secretary's home for long visits, during which the two men took turns telling funny stories and anecdotes. They also took carriage rides together in and around Washington, often viewing the troops and fortifications. In a very short period of time, Seward turned from an attitude of skepticism and mistrust of Lincoln to one of loyalty and admiration.

Interestingly enough, the two men to whom Lincoln became the closest were also the two who originally thought the worst of him. The other was Lincoln's second Secretary of War, Edwin M. Stanton. Despite all of the negative feelings displayed by Stanton, Lincoln still appointed him the new Secretary of War because he knew he was the best man for the job. Lincoln realized that under a somewhat surly exterior existed an honest, devoted, and thoroughly capable administrator. As a result, he let Stanton run the War Department as he saw fit. Often Lincoln signed stack after stack of military commissions that he did not even bother to read. He looked only for Stanton's signature, thinking that if the Secretary had approved them, then they must be all right. When Lincoln died, it was Stanton who muttered, "Now he belongs to the ages." [74]

We can learn from Lincoln's relationships with Seward and Stanton. Simply spending time together and getting to know one's subordinates can overcome mountains of personal differences and hard feelings. If followers learn that their leader is firm, resolute, and committed in the daily performance of his duties, respect can be gained and trust will soon follow.

DON'T SLANDER OR SPREAD GOSSIP

Whoever spreads slander is a fool.
—Proverbs 10:18

Charles Spurgeon knew well how to handle critics: "Suspect those who would lead you to suspect others." [75]

Don't gossip about others; people will distrust your friendship.

Lincoln also spoke on this subject in the context of leadership: "If you once forfeit the confidence of your fellow citizens, you can never regain their respect and esteem." [76]

Leaders who allow their agenda to be set by those least qualified to do so (their critics) have allowed the purpose God has for them to be hijacked toward oblivion. How many—myself included—have spent too much time and energy attempting to keep the critics happy?

We can't allow our agendas to be set by those least qualified to do so—our critics.

I have concluded that trying to keep the critics happy is impossible. They will never be satisfied. Their only joy comes from the morbid practice of criticizing. Slander is a bottomless pit. In fact, James said the tongue is set on fire from the bottomless abyss, hell itself (James 3:6).

Benjamin Franklin, the eighteenth century American printer, author, diplomat, philosopher, and scientist, whose many contributions to the cause of the American Revolution and the newly formed federal government that followed rank him among America's greatest statesmen, said, "I will speak ill of no man, and speak all the good I know of everybody." [77]

SMILE

Great leaders are uplifting. We laugh with people and greet them with genuine smiles. There's something inspirational and memorable about meeting true leaders. Others should feel better after spending time with us.

There's no limit to when we should smile:

❖ We smile when we meet people.

❖ We smile when we answer the phone.

❖ We smile when we stand on a stage.

❖ We smile when we write a letter.

❖ We smile at mistakes.

We must rid ourselves of the frown. A frown is the reflection of a condemning attitude, and it attracts no one at all, except the Devil. Remember that we are relaxing when we smile. It takes fewer facial muscles to smile than it does to frown. Every time we smile, we're etching happy lines on our faces. Let's grow old with these lines of joy rather than lines of worry revealing too much of a miserable life.

The light of the eyes rejoices the heart, and a good report makes the bones healthy. (Proverbs 15:30)

A smile says, "I like you. You make me happy. I am glad to see you." I think this is the reason so many of us have dogs for pets. They are so glad to see us that we become glad to see them, even though they stink, shed hair, cost money, and don't really do anything constructive around the home except some backyard excavation. In spite of all this, we continue to keep them for the glad, happy welcome they give every time we come home—that uncomplicated, smiling company that only a dog can give.

Professor James McConnell, a psychologist at the University of Michigan, stated, "People who smile tend to manage, teach, and sell more effectively, and to raise happier children." [78] I asked a very wealthy man once what he considered to be his key to success. His answer: "If I'm not having fun doing it, then I don't do it." People rarely succeed at anything unless they enjoy what they are doing.

We don't get a second chance to make a first impression.

You must have a good time meeting people if they are to have a good time meeting you. An ancient Chinese proverb says, "Man without smiling face must not open shop." [79]

A smile costs nothing but gives much.
It enriches those who receive
Without impoverishing those who give it.
It takes but a moment,
yet the memory of it sometimes lasts forever.
None is so rich or mighty that he can get along without it,
And none is so poor that he cannot be made rich by it.
A smile creates happiness in the home,
fosters goodwill in business,
and is the countersign of friendship.

A smile brings rest to the weary,
cheer to the discouraged, sunshine to the sad,
and is nature's best antidote for trouble.
Yet it cannot be bought, begged, borrowed, or stolen,
For it is something that is of no value at all
Until it is given away,
And if you meet someone who is too weary
to give you a smile,
leave one of yours.
For no one needs a smile quite so much
as he who has none left to give. [80]
—Author Unknown

PRESENT YOURSELF WELL

Dress in a way that shows respect for the people you are meeting. Dress well for your spouse, for your work, for whatever the occasion. If in doubt, dress one level up, not down.

People opposed to this thinking sometimes say that God doesn't judge us by our clothes but rather by the heart. While this is true, He is the only one who does! What else do we have to measure people by when we first meet them except their appearance and the way they present themselves? We don't make all our judgments on this, but there is no doubt that the way we present ourselves conveys our approach to life.

If I'm feeling good about myself and I have a decent amount of self-respect, it is evident from the way I present myself. My sense of self-respect is readily apparent when I meet you, look you in the eye, and we both feel good with a firm handshake. It only takes six seconds to form the first impression, and then we've both got opinions about each other. We don't get a second chance to make a first impression. We treat each other like children of the Most High God because that's what we know we are on the inside.

I live a certain way because of self-respect. I talk a certain way for the same reason. I leave certain words out of my vocabulary because I respect myself enough to know the boundaries of acceptability and rejection. I make certain choices because of self-respect. I will not dishonor or sully this man made in the image of God. I'm happy with him.

A mistake is an opportunity to learn and train, not criticize and blame.

The heart of the problem is a problem of the heart. Deep inside, my heart must enjoy being me. I take me with me everywhere I go. This is obviously unavoidable. If I catch a plane to Greece, go to a party, become a millionaire, try to be someone else somewhere else, I only find that I'm there, too. I will be coming along with me everywhere I go. I have got to start enjoying being this person God has made, and it shows in the way I walk and the way I talk and the way I present myself in this world.

Be Patient

Great leaders are patient with people. If we're getting exasperated, we don't show it.

> *And a servant of the Lord must not quarrel but be gentle to all, able to teach, patient, in humility correcting those who are in opposition, if God perhaps will grant them repentance, so that they may know the truth.*
> (2 Timothy 2:24–25)

We cover for others: *"Love covers over all wrongs"* (Proverbs 10:12 NIV). We don't remind them of sins or mistakes. We extend ready forgiveness. We're always merciful with people. When people have failed us in some way, we tell them, "It's OK, people make mistakes."

A mistake is an opportunity to learn and train, not criticize and blame.

In 1981, after assuming the reins of the mammoth company General Electric, Jack Welch took the company from assets valued at $20 billion to $272 billion in just twenty years. He freely admits that he and his company have made just about every mistake there is to make. Yet he also says, "Punishing failure assures that no one dares." [81]

At some time in our lives, we all need mercy. If we have shown little, we will receive none when we need it. If we've shown grace, people will be gracious in return when we have made mistakes. And don't be fooled—we all make mistakes.

REPAIR BROKEN RELATIONSHIPS

When a rift occurs in a relationship, fix it! Apologize when you've done wrong. Many fear that an admission of wrong undermines their leadership. In fact, exactly the opposite takes place. We are not so pragmatic and results-oriented that we do this just because we think it will enhance our standing with people. We must do certain things in life just because they're right. We must live by what is right, not just by what our actions will produce.

The other side of repairing relationships is to forgive when others have wronged us. The crucial difference for a kingdom person is that we forgive the wrongs people have done to us before they apologize. We provide an environment of reconciliation and forgiveness. People feel safe to make their apologies.

The Bible says, *"God was in Christ reconciling the world to Himself, not imputing their trespasses to them, and has committed to us the word of reconciliation"* (2 Corinthians 5:19). It is impossible to reconcile people when we are assigning wrongs to their account.

I was shocked while reading Richard Wurmbrand's small book *Sermons in Solitary Confinement.*[82] Locked up in solitary confinement in a cell thirty feet below ground for three years in Bucharest, Wurmbrand questioned God over a number of matters that troubled him. However, he also arrived at some amazing conclusions; the most startling to me was that mature Christians don't forgive!

The quality of repentance is determined by the quality of the environment of forgiveness we provide.

As I read on, I started to understand what he was saying. His view is that if we are living in the kind of love Paul wrote about in 1 Corinthians 13, then love does not even take into account any wrong that it suffers, so it has no need to forgive! This is the fullness of the life of Christ in us. We grow into this realm of the love of God by living in forgiveness.

However, most of us feel the offense when it happens, and we therefore come to God and have to choose to forgive those who have wronged us. This is before they have apologized. They may never apologize, but we will have forgiven them.

In Luke 15, when the Prodigal Son was returning home, he could easily have been imagining his father running toward him with some weapon, about to chase him off the property. The boy had smeared the reputation of the family, spent at least one-third of his father's hard-earned money, and deeply disappointed his father's hopes and aspirations for his son. Nevertheless, his father welcomed him home with a kiss and showered him with abundance. The boy expressed his deep shame and sorrow. The father restored to him all that he had lost.

> **If we place ourselves beyond correction, we place ourselves beyond protection.**

Carrying grudges poisons our attitudes, harms our psychological well-being, and affects our physical health. Forgiving people is a choice we make daily. It is a serious part of the Lord's Prayer. In fact, just after Jesus had taught the disciples this prayer, He again mentioned the need to forgive others so that we can enjoy the forgiveness of our Father in heaven. If we fail to forgive others, we live blocked off from the forgiveness of God and become open to torment (Matthew 18:34–35).

When people make mistakes, it is "we" who made them. When people achieve great results, it is "they" who did it.

CORRECT PEOPLE—WHEN THEY NEED IT

Correction is a part of life. We both receive it and give it in order to be effective leaders.

> *A fool despises his father's instruction, but he who receives correction is prudent....Harsh discipline is for him who forsakes the way, and he who hates correction will die.* (Proverbs 15:5, 10)

Poverty and shame will come to him who disdains correction, but he who regards a rebuke will be honored.
(Proverbs 13:18)

When we correct someone, we approach the person privately with an admission of our own faults. We remove the log from our own eye, and then we can see clearly to remove the speck from our friend's. (See Matthew 7:3–5.)

I have three opening lines when I'm attempting to correct a person. The first is, "Do you think that what you're doing is all right?" If they don't get it, but think that they're fine, then I say, "I'm concerned about what you're doing." If they still fail to see where they've gone offtrack, I simply say, "You're actually out of order."

There are definitely times when people need correction. These times are rare, though. Most books dealing with relational skills either don't address this issue or oppose the idea of rebuking altogether. Instead, they attempt to understand psychologically what is happening in the situation.

However, there is no doubt that a rebuke can achieve much more than hours of attempting to understand a person's problem. A sharp word can shake a person up the right way. There are times when a leader needs to let followers know he or she is upset and that certain behavior is unacceptable. Anger must always be on a leash, though. If leaders don't have control over their tempers, they quickly forfeit respect.

twelve

THE LEADER IS A COMMUNICATOR

*A word fitly spoken is like apples of
gold in settings of silver.*
—*Proverbs 25:11*

A great leader is skilled in two kinds of communication: personal conversation and public speaking. Great leaders are always good communicators with both large and small gatherings. They inspire enthusiasm, loyalty, and sacrifice with their words. Something more than information is imparted from a leader as he or she speaks to a gathering. Spiritual dynamism flows among the listeners.

Ineffective communication lies at the base of many failed exploits. Geoffrey Kells, former managing director of CSR Limited, Australia, says, "The weakness [of an organization] is the result of poor communication networks." [83]

The following story humorously illustrates how misunderstandings can develop when communication skills are poor:

> A husband and wife were in court seeking a divorce. "On what grounds do you want a divorce?" the judge asked the wife.
>
> "All over. We have an acre and a half," she said.
>
> "No, no. Do you have a grudge?" the judge replied.
>
> "Yes, sir, fits two cars."
>
> "I need a reason for the divorce," the judge declared. "Does he beat you up?"
>
> "Oh, no, I'm up at six every day to do my exercises. He gets up later."
>
> "Please!" pleaded the exasperated judge, "What is the reason you want a divorce?"
>
> "Oh," she replied, "We can't seem to communicate with each other."

Leadership relies heavily on the ability to articulate the vision.

Here are several skills that are essential for effective communication:

1. HAVE A GENUINE CONCERN FOR THE PEOPLE YOU ARE TALKING TO.

Most people can tell whether we are interested in them or not. Have we understood what their needs are? What are their questions? Do we want to help them or help ourselves?

If my primary concern is to help people, then they can sense it and clearly read it by my actions. They listen. It is evident in what I say and how I say it. If people can wrap it up and take it home, I have succeeded.

2. BE AWARE OF THE CAPACITY OF PEOPLE TO RECEIVE WHAT YOU ARE SAYING.

Poor communicators focus on themselves and their own opinions. Good communicators focus on the response of the people they're talking to. Good communicators are aware of what their body language and their surroundings are saying. The context of what is being said, the setting, and what is being done should all agree: "The medium is the message." [84]

3. MAKE SURE TO SET PEOPLE AT EASE.

If you are nervous, then others are also. If you are comfortable, you will set people at ease. This confidence transmits through solid eye contact, warmth, and a smile. A smile overcomes innumerable communication barriers. It is the international signal of good will that says, "I like you!"

The successful leader is always a great speaker. Those with difficulty in speaking have to become better communicators if they are to lead effectively. Leadership relies heavily on the ability to articulate the vision. The vision must be communicated so that those who hear it are motivated to action, loyalty, and sacrifice. Aspiring to leadership without this skill is almost pointless. The leader must have, or develop, these abilities.

4. USE REPETITION WHEN NECESSARY FOR EFFECTIVE COMMUNICATION.

Sir Winston Churchill declared, "If you have an important point to make, don't try to be subtle or clever. Use a

203

pile driver. Hit the point once. Then come back and hit it again. Then hit it a third time—a tremendous whack." [85]

A leader always has one major message, and this weaves into everything he or she does. It remains the primary focus. A leader is to some degree a prophet, a person with a message. Great leader see things that others don't. They preach it until others can see it as well. Their message supports the mission. A leader is a preacher, a person who communicates the fire of the mission. Not all preachers are leaders, but all great leaders will be preachers of one sort or another.

DON'T TALK, PREACH!

Even if you're not a pastor or minister, you must be a preacher in the sense that you proclaim your message boldly. Here are a few tips for being a successful communicator/preacher.

1. DEVELOP A CAPTIVATING SPEAKING STYLE.

A monotone is monotonous. Everybody is bored to death with a flat voice. Modulate and vary the tone of voice. We work at making ourselves interesting to listen to, like a beautifully presented five-course dinner in a four-star restaurant.

And remember, speed kills, so keep it within the speed limit. Breathe between statements. Savor the taste of truth. Let it glide down to the "innermost parts" of the listener.

2. STOP SHOUTING!

We exhaust people with noise and clamor. They've turned off when we've only been speaking for five minutes. Great communicators use silence as much as noise.

Quiet tones are powerful when contrasted with loudness. We don't just fill the air with words. We allow space. We allow light and dark, soft and hard, high and low.

3. FIT THE MESSAGE TO THE AUDIENCE.

We order our thoughts according to the mental architecture of our listeners. As a pastor, virtually every time I'm preparing a message, I try to think through the mind-set of different people who will be listening. The point of communicating is to be understood. If this doesn't happen, then we have failed. How do we sound in the ears of our hearers?

4. STAY FOCUSED ON THE MESSAGE.

We don't mob our listeners with every thought that crosses our minds. A quick mind has ample opportunity to travel down any number of side streets emerging from the deep morass of gray matter. We remain disciplined in thought and undistracted from our target. We phrase each sentence so that it is like an arrow from the bow of a great archer.

Even if you're not a pastor, you must be a preacher in the sense that you proclaim your message boldly.

We always have in mind the main message we are attempting to convey—this can be helpful and is generally quite important! Everything we say drives the same point home. If you're a pastor, do not attempt to deliver more than one message per sermon. Remember the acronym KISS ("keep it short and sweet"). I have the question, "What are you trying to say?" boldly lettered across the top of my sermon notes when I preach.

5. IMPART PASSION.

We impart the feeling of what we're communicating. Information is not enough. There must be passion and pathos in a leader. Leadership is not just about facts and data—it's about a dream born in the heart, about the communication of fire.

Good communication is the grown-up version of "show and tell."

However, we don't rely on emotional expressions to describe what we're saying. We think in terms and speak with words that leave the listener with emotion. As a pastor, for instance, I don't just put my vocabulary on the shelf and attempt to express myself with, "God is so-o-o-o amazing." Instead, I describe why He is amazing with facts, testimonies, and experiences that leave people with no recourse but to exclaim, "God is amazing!"

TELL STORIES

In communicating, we must be aware that people remember stories. Stories move people because they stir emotions. If you want to be an effective leader, learn to tell stories.

Good communication is the grown-up version of "show and tell." The principle we are teaching should occupy around ten to thirty percent of what we say. The rest needs to be illustration. Telling stories as illustrations cannot be emphasized enough. Jesus used stories as illustrations for almost ninety percent of His preaching.

Many speakers don't know how to illustrate. In today's television and movie world, we have no choice but to accept the mission, "Give 'em pictures." Pictures are something people hang their emotions on. The listener's imagination is our greatest tool. Master this art. Practice, practice, practice.

There are five kinds of illustrations we can use:

1. BIBLICAL STORIES

There's a story on every page of Scripture, and each one illustrates the truth of the Bible in some way or another. Even if you aren't a pastor, biblical stories can still be used as illustrations in communicating to those you lead.

As we study the surrounding culture, customs, and facts of a story, we can grasp the background. Then it's easy to use imagination. We tie the truth and the background together and create a story.

I love taking a Scripture passage and researching the background to arrive at an exciting story that emphasizes the truth I'm sharing. At our recent Easter services, we saw a lot of people receive Christ. It was Easter, and I was telling a modern-day version of the story of Jesus raising the widow of Nain's son (Luke 7:11–15).

> A young couple, Matthew and Elizabeth, were getting married after three years of courting. Finally their wedding day had come. They had spent hours together at the sidewalk café planning their future, sharing their dreams, sketching out what kind of house they would build, and deciding how many children they would have. He was twenty and she was just eighteen. They had already saved and purchased a condo down at Lake Galilee, and so they moved in right after the wedding. Time passed and Matthew was promoted. He earned good money as the foreman out at the forestry.

He walked into the house one evening, and Elizabeth looked at him in a really strange way with a funny smile on her face. She had been to the doctor earlier. Matthew's heart leapt as he realized his little lady was going to bring their baby into the world. Time passed and little Johnny was born. He grew into a fine young lad. He was five years old and off to school already.

One day there was an urgent knock on the door. Elizabeth ran to the door to answer it. A policeman was standing there. He told her to come with him. There was an accident at the forest, and her husband might have been involved. They arrived at the end of a dirt track in the forest where several men were crowded around a fallen tree. The policeman escorted Elizabeth to the scene. There, underneath the tree, was a crumpled figure. She crouched down and reached out her hand. She recognized the face of her husband. He was lifeless and cold. She stood up, her head spinning. She fainted and slipped to the ground. Later, she remembered lights flashing and sirens, and then she was home again. Friends came by.

Little Johnny was just coming home from school. She scooped him up in her arms, sobbing and sobbing. She poured all her feelings into her little boy. Someone gave her a sedative, and together they fell asleep in each other's arms. She awoke, thinking it had been a terrible nightmare, but then realized that it was true. Her friends were still in the house. The funeral arrangements had been made. She went through the motions of the funeral without much feeling at all. She was numb with grief.

Their wounds healed over a period of time. Young Johnny grew up to be a strong, mature young man.

Elizabeth didn't remarry. The whole town of Nain admired the courage of the woman, and all thought highly of the young man, who was now the spitting image of his father. John had recently gotten his driver's license. Mom had saved enough to help him buy a car. He was off with his friends. Over the weekend, they were going to take a long drive around the lake. It was 7 p.m. and he hadn't arrived back yet. "He should have called," she thought. He had a cell phone. It was 9 p.m. She was worried.

There's a story on every page of Scripture illustrating the truth of the Bible in some way or another.

There was a knock on the door. A policeman stood there. Dark memories flooded her mind. They drove to a car wreck just one mile down the road. There at the intersection, she looked at the lifeless body of her only boy—her only reason for living.

She screamed into the sky. She didn't know if she was furious beyond words or completely heartbroken. Elizabeth couldn't understand why God had allowed such a thing. All she could imagine was taking her own life.

The funeral was planned for the next day. It was the blackest night of her life. The doctor sedated her. Around midday the next day, a great funeral procession of hundreds of people dressed in black moved slowly out through the gates of the city. Almost the entire town had come out in sympathy for the woman and the boy they had all grown to love so much.

Meanwhile, another procession was making its way toward the gates of the city. Hundreds of people were all dressed in colorful clothes, moving quickly, dust everywhere, singing and chattering. At the front was a group of happy young men surrounding a determined-looking noble person, who strode with purpose toward the procession of death coming out of the city.

The procession of life met the procession of death.

Leading the procession of life was a living man, Jesus Christ. The reason His followers were so full of life was because He Himself was alive. He approached the coffin. He told them to remove the lid, even though it would stink of death and decay. He touched the boy. Just one touch from the Lord was all it took for resurrection life to fill the boy's body. He spoke, "Young man, get up."

That's the call to young people everywhere. Young person, let the resurrection power of Christ fill your life, and get up! Go!

2. FICTITIOUS STORIES

Another type of illustration is a fictitious story. A parable is a story that we invent—something from our own imagination with fictitious characters and fictitious circumstances—that illustrates a point. One of the easiest ways to do this is to give life and personality to inanimate things, like the wind, the ocean, or the trees. Giving them names and using their unique qualities helps describe our point.

I have a number of characters I have invented who work well in many stories. Joe Christian is a guy who seems to say all the right things but never actually does them. He prays every day that God will use him, but he doesn't witness to his secretary when she's crying or his boss when he's hung over or his Dad when he's depressed. He doesn't help Sister Brown home with her groceries from the supermarket, or he forgets he was giving a lift to someone to get them to church. He watches TV all night and forgets to go to church. He spends his tithe on a drill he doesn't really need, and so on.

3. HUMOROUS STORIES

There are some great jokes that serve to help people wash down what we're trying to communicate. Jokes need to have a point if they are part of a message.

Winston Churchill was known for a rapier-like wit and was famous for some great comebacks, such as the time when a major political opponent met him in the hallway but continued to march straight toward Winston, declaring, "I don't get out of the way of fools," to which the prime minister replied, "But I do," and stepped aside.

Jokes serve to help people wash down what we're trying to communicate.

Concerning humor, Churchill said, "In my belief, you cannot deal with the most serious things in the world unless you also understand the most amusing." [86]

4. ANOTHER'S TESTIMONIES

Testimonies can help prove points we are making. Because of the need to constantly acquire a vast library of stories, we must read and read and read.

5. PERSONAL EXAMPLES

Think of the things God has done for you that show the truth you're communicating. Probably the quickest way to gain people's attention is to talk about our personal lives. Anything about our own world, especially where we've messed up or something that's pretty funny about our own lives, helps listeners relate to what we're saying. The things we do with our families, with our spouse, with our spare time on vacation—all help us to relate well to those we are leading. We've got to let people into our world.

MAJOR ON MAJORS, NOT ON MINORS

Some communicators occupy themselves with trivial matters, consuming great energy and time on obscure and irrelevant matters. This is like a lion chasing mice, especially for a preacher of the Word of God. Leave chasing mice for the cats; lions have greater issues to deal with.

There are just a few great basic truths we must deal with. These must be said again and again in a thousand different ways. The six truths of the sixth chapter of Hebrews—repentance, faith, baptisms, laying on of hands, resurrection, eternal judgment—are more than sufficient to keep us in enough material until we die. If we need anything else, then Paul told us that *"faith, hope, and love"* (1 Corinthians 13:13 NIV) are the three greatest. If we truly believe that the primary purpose presented in the Gospels is to *"make disciples of all the nations"* (Matthew 28:19), then we will resist the temptation to impress others with our ability to derive esoteric meanings from obscure verses.

We don't allow ourselves to be drawn into preaching on matters with no relevance to our listeners. If our sermons can't be taken home and lived out, then they are of no value to anyone.

The Word is not a proof text for a belief system external to its own pages.

Never preach out of petty hurts, personal causes, or personal opinions. Preach in the Holy Spirit, and always *"preach the word!"* (2 Timothy 4:2).

A number of years ago, in the pursuit of understanding management, I familiarized myself with a great variety of available business management materials and a lot of the positive mental attitude books that go along with them. Some of the material found its way into my preaching and teaching. I felt a growing discomfort in my spirit, without really understanding what it was.

One day, as I was reading Deuteronomy 22:9, *"You shall not sow your vineyard with different kinds of seed, lest the yield of the seed which you have sown and the fruit of your vineyard be defiled,"* I realized I could not afford to have a bag of mixed seed. I felt convicted to purify my message so that the material would only reinforce what the Word already says.

The danger here is that if we find ourselves trying to find Scriptures to validate pet theories we are attracted to, we may compromise the power of the Gospel. The Word is not a proof text for a belief system external to its own pages.

This approach to Scripture is dangerous. It is a bag of mixed seed.

We cannot afford to meddle with the Word of God. Peter said that people who *"twist"* the Scriptures, do so *"to their own destruction"* (2 Peter 3:16).

We have a great counseling ministry in our church headed up by a professional psychologist, Julie Crabtree. Julie and her team do an awesome job in training many counselors to deal with scores of needs in people's lives. However, one of the most dangerous areas for distortion of the Scriptures today is in the area of counseling.

We cannot afford to dilute the Word of God, the awesome supernatural force He has given us.

There seem to be a thousand different concepts of what Christian counseling is. Some link together a tenuous structure of Scriptures, attempting to give credence to a concept. Both the concepts of "positive mental attitude" and "counseling" are good in themselves. However, if we find ourselves preaching a concept of the world's thinking and then forcing the meaning of Scripture to suit that theory in order to give it credence, we've mixed our seed and rendered the Word of God minimally effective.

The Word is truth. The Word of God is enough of a message all on its own. The Word is the food God has given us to minister to the believer. It has a power within it to save souls. We cannot afford to dilute this awesome supernatural force God has placed in our hands. The Word of God reveals the blood of Christ to deal with sin through repentance. It reveals that faith in God obtains results, and when this is not the way, then faith supplies us with the ability to make it through whatever we face. The Word of God reveals that sometimes pain and suffering are actually beneficial to the believer, no matter how much positive mental attitude we attempt and no matter how many different kinds of counseling we seek. God uses the pain of some circumstances to change us into the image of Christ. The plans, methods, and desired results of the Word of God are vastly different from those of the world.

As Christians, we are building an eternal kingdom that will never go out of date. We are not attempting to make our message relevant by changing the basic truths or attempting to get the same results through other means. A spiritual kingdom is built with spiritual tools. The kingdom of God is built with the tools Jesus has given us. There's no other way. The Word feeds the spirits of Christians. The church becomes strong and bears fruit because of the Word of God. *"Preach the word!"* (2 Timothy 4:2).

Keep it simple. We don't use language or words not understood by our listeners. We need to be careful not to use concepts, philosophies, or phrases that impress no one else. Our task is not to impress but to deal with the souls of men and women. It is said that John Wesley often first preached his sermons to the maid in his house. He asked her if she understood what he said. Whatever was not understood he changed. "What point," he said, "is there in preaching if the simplest person in the gathering cannot understand what is being said?"

What we preach is what we get. We are farmers sowing seed. If we are unhappy with the harvest we're reaping, we should sow different seed. If we want different results, we preach different messages.

When it comes to Christian leadership, be fearless in bringing about conviction, weeping, and repentance. People need to feel these things, not just know about them. People should be left under the pain of conviction until they break through their resistance to repentance. When we allow this, we do the greatest service to a person anyone can do. We preach the Word of God, causing sinners to become saints, like a surgeon removing sin and implanting Christ Himself into a human life.

thirteen

THE LEADER IS ORGANIZED

Organized people are able to move through life at a fast pace.

O rganization is simple and basic but essential for success. Life comes at us like a thundering herd of wild animals—all the things that must be done, all the things we want to do, all the things others require of us, all the things circumstances thrust upon us—all these demands require that we order our lives so we can deal successfully with everything.

Organization can be reduced to time and place. There is a time for everything. *"To everything there is a season, a time for every purpose under heaven"* (Ecclesiastes 3:1). This is called appropriateness. We work when we're meant to. We rest when we're meant to. We plan our time so that we spend it on our highest pursuits and the things we value most.

Organization is all about systems. For lack of a better term, systems are "habits." When I was a child, we were required to change the bed sheets every Thursday morning. That was the day the sheets and towels were washed in our house. These were habits everyone had to acquire. This and other habits formed systems, and the household operated smoothly. The whole family knew the system, and we worked with the system. This gave us the security and clarity of knowing what was required of us and when.

This anonymous poem says it well:

> You may know me.
> I'm your constant companion.
> I'm your greatest helper.
> I'm your heaviest burden.
> I will push you onward or drag you down to failure.
> I am at your command.
> Half the tasks you do might as well be turned over to me.
> I'm able to do them quickly,
> And I'm able to do them the same every time if
>   that's what you want.
> I'm easily managed—all you've got to do is be
>   firm with me.
> Show me exactly how you want it done,
> And after a few lessons I'll do it automatically.
> I am the servant of all great men and women,
> Of course, servant of the failures as well.
> I've made all the great men who have ever been great.
> And I've made all the failures, too.
> But I work with all the precision of a marvelous computer,
>   With the intelligence of a human being.
> You may run me for profit or you may run me to ruin;
>   It makes no difference to me.
> Take me.
> Be easy with me, and I will destroy you.
> Be firm with me, and I'll put the world at your feet.
> Who am I?
> I'm HABIT! [87]

Management must have basic systems in order to operate smoothly. Systems synchronize time and place among people in a group.

Place is also crucial to organization. If the idea of place is not understood, we waste time. The hammer "lives" in a certain place. When we've used it, we return it to its place. We file things, not only to put them out of sight, but so we can retrieve them again when we want them. We waste time looking for the hammer when it's not in its place. This is the same with the keys or our wallet or our sunglasses or whatever.

Our time is our life! When we waste time, we are wasting our life!

What is time? Our time is our life! When we waste time, we are wasting our life!

While we're searching for the hammer, we could be doing something with it. When we're looking for the keys, time is passing that shouldn't be. People live frustrated and unproductive lives because they are unorganized. Things don't have "place" in their lives.

PUNCTUALITY

If you're always early, you'll never be late! Don't waste other people's time. Being punctual is essential if we want respect from others. Everyone feels his or her time is precious—and it is! Tardiness is a serious character flaw. It is not a light issue, even though perpetually tardy people think it is.

If ten people are on time and the eleventh is thirty minutes late, things can't happen until that last person arrives. The result is that five hours of other people's lives have been wasted because of someone's tardiness. Always be early, and you're sure to impress. Tardiness doesn't create trust. However, promptness demonstrates respect as well as earns it. People realize they can rely on you.

David Yonggi Cho leads the largest church in the world, yet he makes sure he's always early for appointments. I've heard him say he tries to be fifteen minutes early for any appointment. If anyone has an excuse for lateness, he does. This reveals one of the reasons why this man has developed enough trust for such a large church and team to grow up around him.

Promptness demonstrates respect as well as earns it.

The worst thing about disorganized people is that they fail to see how frustrating they are to themselves and to others. They laugh a tittering giggle, saying things like, "Oh, I'm so disorganized, aren't I?" Everyone rolls their eyes, nods their head, and wonders what planet these people are from.

Watching an unorganized person make breakfast is a hair-pulling event. He puts cereal in the bowl, pours the milk in, finds a spoon, and then eats. Then he thinks some toast would be good to have, so he gets bread out of the bin, puts the toaster out on the counter, sticks a slice in the toaster slot, and waits for it to brown. Sproing! Up it pops. Look for the butter. No butter! Off to the corner market to get some butter. Oops, no money in the wallet! Off to the ATM. Get cash, go back to the store, buy the butter, and go home again. Oops, no honey or jam either! Back to the store, but where did I put my keys? Finally, get the honey and return home. Put the toast back in to reheat. Now, he's ready—almost. Some coffee would be nice with his toast. So half an hour later he has the coffeepot going, and he watches it drip. Finally around dinnertime, he's managed to finish breakfast. Only a foolhardy person would even think about asking this kind of guy to mail a letter for them.

Don Argus, managing director of the National Australia Bank, believes that time management is critical to effective leadership. He takes time every morning to prioritize the daily demands so that he can dictate his own pace. [88]

Organized people are able to move at a fast pace through life. They have fluidity and motion in their lives. They are able to keep a hundred things going at once. The sheer energy and dynamism of all the things happening simultaneously creates an updraft of energy and excitement for everyone around them.

THE METHODS AND ART OF ORGANIZATIONAL SKILLS

Being organized is being methodical. This can mean solving problems by process of elimination. Tackle a task one step at a time. Don't try to do everything at once. Do first things first. When we systemize our lives, we accomplish tasks faster and more completely than in any other way.

I have systems for almost every area of my life. About ninety percent of the time, my life is actually quite predictable. If I keep myself working within a system, I find I am able to achieve at a far higher level.

Creative people may squirm at this thought in the erroneous belief that a spontaneous life is the only way to let true creativity rise. This isn't true though. I recently read about Ken Done, one of Australia's leading artists, and how he goes to work on his paintings at 9 a.m. each day, works until 5 or 6 p.m., and then finishes.

I am involved in writing songs, preparing sermons, and painting paintings, all highly creative processes. In fact, had I not entered the ministry, I was going to be an artist. I find I can organize the execution of creative ideas so that my world remains orderly and I can keep accomplishing things at higher levels. Creative surges come spontaneously, but even these times can be organized by making sure I've arranged the setting for creativity to flow easily.

Even though we're talking about little things like making breakfast and mailing letters, these apparently simple systems, when applied to the way we approach the work of our organizations, will translate into success or failure. The winning or losing of business, the growing or shrinking of a church, or the gain or loss of millions of dollars could be at stake. Organization means success or failure.

PLANS

"We should make plans—counting on God to direct us" (Proverbs 16:9 TLB).

Donald Trump, the New York property developer who has amassed, lost, and then recovered vast fortunes in real estate deals involving billions of dollars, says, "Wait patiently for right opportunities to get what you want and then move quickly. Be extremely efficient. Fight all the way for costs and excellence to be maintained." [89]

People who live life by an organized game plan are always in a better position to take advantage of opportunities when they arise. If we're not in position on the field when the ball is being passed, we're not going to catch it. If we're in the right position at the right time, the chance to score does not pass us by.

If we're not in position on the field when the ball is being passed, we're not going to catch it.

This means we are keeping up with the game. We are on the field. We're a player. We are at the events. We are in contact and keeping connected. We organize communication and plan meetings. We know that winning never just "happens."

THREE FACTORS OF PROJECT ORGANIZATION

Every project we ever embark upon must have three factors in place:

- ❖ Authorities
- ❖ Designs
- ❖ Resources

In the early days of starting a church, I began with very naïve ideas about how to get into a building to house the church. I was thinking it was simply a matter of finding the right facility, organizing the money, and moving in.

However, I found the local civic authorities had different ideas. We found a building, but they wouldn't approve us using it as a church until we had made a huge amount of changes to it. These threatened to cost enormous sums of money. The changes had to meet our needs, satisfy council requirements, and fit into a budget.

I have been involved in numerous building projects since that time. Now we always address these matters first whenever the overseeing committee or board meets. We report on our progress with authorities, designs, and resources.

These three factors are not limited only to building projects, either. They apply to everything we attempt to do.

Always make sure to define the need before designing the answer.

Do we have the necessary authority to do what we are planning? Has God said, "Do it"? Have those we're accountable to agreed to the plans? Are other authorities on board? Do we have agreement from other people who are important to the project being successful—our family, friends, neighbors, congregation, employees and management team, and relevant governmental agencies?

Do our plans meet the needs we have? There's little point in designing a building, hiring a person, or planning a function that doesn't meet the need. Define the need before designing the answer. Some people are busy answering questions nobody is asking or meeting needs that people don't have. Obviously, a comprehensive understanding of need must precede design. We must have it clear in our minds what we are trying to accomplish.

Resources are such things as money, time, people, and circumstances. Do we have the resources to succeed? Do we have the money? Will the bank lend the money? Do we have the people? Do we have the time? Do we have the skills, experience, and knowledge available to accomplish it? If not, then we should make sure these are in place before we start so that we are not embarrassed and the work of God is not maligned:

> For which of you, intending to build a tower, does not sit down first and count the cost, whether he has enough to finish it; lest, after he has laid the foundation, and is not able to finish, all who see it begin to mock him, saying, "This man began to build and was not able to finish."
> (Luke 14:28–30)

Lack of preparation is a sure way to fail. Preparation is always the hard part of success.

WINNING

People have come to believe that winning is just a matter of luck. People around the world spend billions of dollars every year gambling, whether they are betting on the horses or their favorite pro team, or are throwing away their money at casinos or on lotteries.

The highest levels of success are not matters of luck. Success is the result of hard work, organization, great people skills, the willingness to continue learning, confidence, and committing all our works into the hands of God.

Many Christians still imagine that success is something that falls out of the sky. We imagine that trucks will back up to our houses and pour out all the furniture we need. We think it is coming in the mail—our big lucky break from God, of course. But winning does not come like that. Winning occurs because we do all we can to ensure it will come about by working hard, by right preparation, and by making wise decisions. God blesses our efforts, not our wishes.

One of the most successful coaches in American football history, Vince Lombardi, who in the 1960s led the Green Bay Packers to five National Football League victories and on to two Super Bowl championships, has said, "Winning is a habit. Unfortunately, so is losing." [90]

The timeless story of David and Goliath (see 1 Samuel 17) reveals at least nine principles of winning.

1. BE FEARLESS.

Fear paralyzes action and thought. The Israelites were frozen with fear. Not a blow had been delivered, yet for six weeks, no one had engaged in battle. The bellowing taunts of the freakish-looking giant held an entire army ransom to terror. Problems always bellow failure in our faces. Yet, filled with the Holy Spirit and boldness from heaven, we can achieve the same as David. Our aim is to paralyze fear before it paralyzes us.

2. STAY FAITHFUL.

David would never have had the opportunity had he not been trustworthy. His father entrusted him with the job of taking supplies to his brothers. He was also organized and trustworthy enough to arrange for his other responsibilities to be cared for while he was gone. He made sure his flock of sheep would be in good hands in his absence. He was also to bring back news regarding his brothers. Jesse, David's father, knew David could be relied on to bring back a full report.

3. FOCUS.

When David's older brothers heard his bold response to the giant's challenge, they accused him of meddling where he was uninvited. They condemned him as arrogant and full of pride. Yet David had a vision that he could actually defeat the hulk.

If we know we can achieve our vision, we tell it to the people who matter and those who can believe with us. David was brilliant in presenting his vision. He convinced Saul, the king of Israel, that he could deliver the entire nation from impending bondage to the Philistines, even though he had never fought in a national battle or been trained in the art of war. Saul actually entrusted the future of the entire nation and his own position as king into the hands of the brave young warrior, who didn't appear to have grown enough to be a soldier. Yet David's argument held enough conviction to compel Saul to hand the fate of his country into a battle between this shepherd lad and the Philistine champion.

> **If we know we can achieve our vision, we tell it to the people who matter.**

4. RELY ON EXPERIENCE.

Recall past experiences when you have proven that you can overcome in equally threatening, even if not as significant, circumstances. The testimony of the young shepherd to the king was a most compelling communication. David had already shown his valor by defeating a lion and a bear. He knew he could do it. This is where conviction comes from. We know it can be done because we have previously succeeded. This again highlights our need for personal, private victory.

5. BE YOURSELF.

Don't be afraid to think outside the box of convention. There are normal ways to fight a war and to fight a giant.

David didn't fit another man's armor, methods, or strategies. Saul offered the young man the king's own armor, but it was too big, and David was unsure in it. He attempted to do as his king requested but declined after it was obviously unsuitable.

However, David did know his own ways, and his faith was in God and in being himself. He had already figured out how the giant was to be beaten. The sling and the stone would do the job. He was fully confident he would find his mark with the first missile. No one had even considered this as a strategy.

Don't be afraid to think outside the box of convention.

We don't let the Devil dictate the terms of the battle. We fight the Enemy on our terms, on our turf. This is where our victory is.

One of the unique qualities of our fellowship of churches and ministers is the great diversity that exists among us. Hamish and Dianne Divett oversee the movement in New Zealand. Their church is wonderfully unique, and the Sunday services are packed because they have held to a fresh approach to church worship and culture. Among other things, they have developed an inspiring counseling technique, through which many people are discovering release and new freedom. Yet they have also encountered criticism, simply because it employs new language and methods that are unfamiliar to most.

Basically, their method is that it helps people find God in their lives using questions such as, "Where is God for you?"

and "What does that feel like?" This is a unique expression of who they are in Christ, and as they have remained true to that expression, they have discovered the blessing of God on their ministry.

6. PROPHESY.

David spoke to Goliath and prophesied what, when, and how he would defeat the giant and the entire Philistine army. Instead of speaking *about* our problems, we need to speak *to* them. Even though the Enemy has issued threats and proclamations of victory of his own, they are futile against the promises of God. The Word of God prevails every time over the feeble threats of an already defeated enemy.

7. DO IT FOR GOD.

David's motivation was jealousy for the honor of Yahweh. He was incensed at the mocking of the giant. David's aim was to bring God the glory.

If we are living for God and seeking *"first the kingdom of God and His righteousness"* (Matthew 6:33), we will find all the resources of heaven are at our disposal. The choices we make in life need to be for God, not for ourselves. The battles we fight need to be battles for God and for His glory. Let's not find ourselves fighting battles God is not involved in. Fight the fight for His glory. We will discover strategies that yield victory every time.

8. DON'T HESITATE.

David ran to the giant. Once he committed himself to the strategy, he was unhesitant. He knew he was going to win, and he knew exactly how. Starting is always halfway to winning. The start always needs to be bold and decisive. Great leaders make their decisions and then commit fully to making them happen.

9. COMPLETE THE TASK.

David didn't do just half the job; he completed it by severing the head of the Philistine champion. He finished what he had to do. The stone imbedded itself in the forehead of the giant, but this only rendered the champion unconscious. David continued to run to the giant. With Goliath's own sword, David removed the great head of the monster.

TIME

In *King Richard II*, Shakespeare's Richard lamented, "I wasted time and now doth time waste me." [91]

Let's not find ourselves fighting battles God is not involved in.

Given my age and the current lifespan projections, I have another 35 years or so on this earth—that's 12,740 days. One-third of that time I'll be sleeping. At least another third I'll be doing things ancillary to the main purposes of my life. That leaves me with about 4,000 days to give myself to my priorities. It is seriously important that I don't waste this time I have. Time is a gift of God, more precious than gold.

Both Paul and King David understood the value of time. These verses tell us that it is a wise person who arranges life to maximize time:

> *So teach us to number our days, that we may gain a heart of wisdom.* (Psalm 90:12)

*See then that you walk circumspectly, not as fools but
as wise, redeeming the time, because the days are evil.
Therefore do not be unwise, but understand what the
will of the Lord is.*   (Ephesians 5:15–17)

Troubled days subtract precious time from our lives.
We are distracted from dealing with the issues that really
matter. Therefore, we must take advantage of every
moment in our lives.

PLAN YOUR TIME

Probably the most common complaint people have is
that they have no time. The trouble with that complaint
is that everyone on earth has exactly the same amount
of time. Some are accomplishing enormous things with
theirs; others are doing nothing at all. The problem is
not with "having" enough time; rather, it has to do with
"making" time and "organizing" the time we have.

Making time is simple. We simply plan it. If we don't,
the priceless resource of time slips quietly through our
fingers until we reach the end of our lives, and it's all
gone.

How do we plan? We write our schedule down in a
daily diary. When the time arrives to do something, we
simply do it. When less important things try to usurp our
time, we've pre-organized the higher priority items so that
we have a previous appointment we must keep.

I'm constantly amazed at the relative unimportance of
almost everything. There are very few things in this world
that are really important. Most of what screams out that
it can't wait actually can. Running around trying to fulfill
everyone else's demands is not going to give us the success

we're looking for. We prioritize our time according to our priorities in life. The comedian and actor Bill Cosby tapped into the importance of priorities when he said,

> **I don't know the secret to success, but the secret to failure is trying to please everybody.** [92]
> **—Bill Cosby**

We also make time by not spending time on futile things. I don't have the time to read the newspapers every day. Some might, but I don't, and frankly, I don't need to. If I were a politician, I might need to, but I'm not, so reading the Word has a higher priority. I read the Saturday morning paper and watch the six o'clock news headlines about three times during the week, and that keeps me up-to-date and informed.

There are very few things in this world that are really important.

I don't have time to read novels, watch an endless array of movies, or go to every social event we're invited to either. There are more important things I'm living for than endless small talk and late nights doing nothing. I'm not trying to find things to do. I have reprioritized all the things I'm not going to do so I have time to do those things I must do—and do them as well as I can.

Make Lists

Organized people live by lists. List the important things you are to do today, this week, this year, and this life, and then do the most important things first.

People without lists find life overwhelming. When we go shopping, we make a list of the things we need. We mark them off as we get each item on the list. When we're doing a job with many different tasks involved, we have a list and mark off each task as it's completed. We have lists of today's goals, this year's goals, and our life goals.

Create to-do lists, goal lists, problem lists, fault lists, sin lists—so you can view what needs to be dealt with and then deal with it. If an army approaches you like a wall, they will be difficult to defeat; but if you line the members of an army up in single file, you'll find you can knock them over one by one.

Plan from the completion of the goal backward. Start from the finish. We always ask ourselves, "What am I attempting to achieve?" "What do I want to happen?" We find the answers to these questions then we devise a plan to bring us to that point. This is "results orientation." It keeps us from just doing the job or playing the game without being concerned about the results. It matters little how hard or long we work or how talented we are at the game. Did we get the results? Did we win the game? Did we achieve what we set out to do?

A good example of poor execution of this principle is the story of the city workmen who pulled up their truck outside the house of a retired gentleman. One of the workers jumped out and dug a hole. Then the other workman got out and filled it in. The old-timer was sitting on his porch watching this with fascination.

The workmen drove a little further down the street. Again one jumped out and dug another hole. The other then got out again and filled it in. They drove a little further and proceeded to do the same.

The old-timer's fascination turned to frustration when he remembered that he paid taxes to employ these guys. He walked down to the men and asked, "What the heck are you doing, digging a hole and then filling it up again?" They replied, "The guy who plants the trees is sick today!"

That is what happens when people are completely unconcerned with end results and are just there to do their job. People may be able to kick a ball around a field with amazing skill. Who cares? Do they score goals?

Organized people live by lists, while people without lists find life overwhelming.

I don't approach Sundays with an attitude of, "What message shall I preach?" but rather, "What do we want to achieve in our church at this time?" That desired end result determines what and how I preach. Then, within the particular message, I ask myself, "What am I trying to achieve here? What one thing am I attempting to say? What do I want these people to have or do at the end of this time?'

Then I follow the plan. A plan always has exciting parts to it, especially at the beginning, but then comes the hard chores you have to slog through. Tackle the hard parts first. Anything worthwhile takes longer, demands a higher price, and encounters stronger opposition than you thought it would. Cover the hard yards so you can enjoy the easy parts without thinking you've yet to tackle the difficult areas.

The elementary school I attended as a child supplied a sit-down lunch every day. Mostly the food was pretty terrible. The vegetables were really bad—stringy carrots, wooden parsnips, and soggy cabbage—but we had to eat it all. So I made myself eat the vegetables first, then get down to the meat.

Get the hard parts, the distasteful parts, over and done with first, and then the end is far more enjoyable. Leave the good bits until the end. It's a reward. It's a part of the inspiration that you need to keep going with the tough stuff, because you know the good part is yet to come. If the good part is already all over, you're not that inspired to keep going.

Be thorough in the planning stages. Don't be impatient to get to the finish. The old carpenter's rule is "measure twice, cut once." Do it properly the first time, and you won't have to do it a second or a third. Cover all the bases in the planning stage, and the execution will be child's play.

To prepare well takes time, but to repair afterward takes much more. The results of not doing a thing properly have disastrous effects. In two or three of the battles lost in the American Civil War, the result is said to have been due to bad gunpowder that was supplied to the army by shoddy contractors.

The Boy Scout motto still applies: "Be prepared." It's amazing how many people need to borrow things from others simply because they didn't get themselves ready for an event. In the parable of the ten virgins, Jesus addressed the problem of not getting ready in relation to the Second Coming. Obviously, that's a fairly large event to make sure we're ready for. On less of a grand scale though, each day we should be prepared for whatever arises.

Prepared people don't need to be bothered with the basics all the time; they have pens in their pockets, paper to write on, money in their wallets, sunglasses, full tanks of gas, maps in the car, and a jacket for the weather. It goes on and on. The person who doesn't think ahead is always at a supreme disadvantage to anyone else who does. Whether it's leadership, church ministry, sales, or business negotiations, the prepared person is always in front.

"I'm convinced that achieving success for an individual or company requires no more and no less than paying serious attention to 'first things.' Most people aren't willing to put first things first." [93]

Get the hard parts, the distasteful parts, over and done with first, and then the end is far more enjoyable.

Do things when you're asked, not when they are due. This way you're always ahead of yourself and completely prepared. When the assignment is due in four weeks' time, start it immediately. Don't wait four weeks and then do it the night before it's due. That lifestyle creates high stress.

Always get the work done before you play. Work before play—always! Once the work is completed, then play. Your "play" will be free of guilt and stress.

The only thing preventing people from being organized—if they have implemented these habits in their lives—is discipline. Grit your teeth and make yourself stick with the plan. Stick with your commitments. Stick with them until the list is clear. Don't follow your emotions; live by principles, plans, priorities, and purpose.

DIMENSIONS OF TIME

Time has three dimensions—the past, the present, and the future. We must have each under control, and in that order. If the past is not properly dealt with, it destabilizes our present and destroys our future. If our present isn't being dealt with properly, our future has no platform for take-off.

With finances, for example, if bills from the past aren't paid, we are unable to invest in the future. If we are not paying the rent on our house or on our office for the present, we've got nowhere to live or to do business from in the future. Having a vision for the future is great, but some of us need to get a vision of our past in order to fix it up.

Others of us need visions for the present; we need to arrange our lives so they work in the here and now. Sometimes we can be caught using a vision for the future as an escape from the consequences of the past and the responsibilities of the present. As we deal with the past and the present, we're able to move forward into the future.

I've watched people leave their jobs, trying to start up a company or even a church. They believe it's all going to work so well that they can leave what they're doing and have instant success. The best way to venture out into a new thing is to keep a steady paying job so that the rent, food, and other basics of life are covered. This means working harder. It may mean working after hours into the night. This is the price of getting out in front. Nothing great comes without a price.

Finish your outdoor work and get your fields ready;
after that, build your house.   (Proverbs 24:27 NIV)

PLACE

Being organized means understanding that everything has a place, right down to the car keys. We rob ourselves, our employees, and our businesses of days and weeks every year because we can't find things as simple as car keys. While we're looking for keys or whatever else is misplaced, we could be doing something far more productive.

All it takes is having a place for each thing to "live" and making sure to keep things where they live. We put things back when we've used them. When we walk out of the house in the morning, we have all we need for the day with us. This is a ritual every morning so that we're not always asking to borrow someone else's things. It means we don't waste time or money getting a ticket for not having our driver's license on us or borrowing money because we haven't got our wallet.

We rob ourselves and others entire weeks every year because we can't find things as simple as car keys.

Such time-wasters are frustrating for everybody around us. The consequences of living with an unfocused mind are that we're frustrated with ourselves, huffing and puffing as we look for keys, yelling at our kids because we're upset, and generally feeling overwhelmed. In approaching life this way, we live far below our potential simply because we did not get organized.

In his book *Margin: Restoring Emotional, Physical, Financial, and Time Reserves to Overloaded Lives,* Dr. Richard Swenson stated,

Marginless is being thirty minutes late to the doctor's office because you were twenty minutes late getting out of the hairdressers, because you were ten minutes late dropping the children off at school because the car ran out of gas two blocks from the gas station—and you forgot your purse. Margin, on the other hand, is having breath left at the top of the staircase, money left at the end of the month, and sanity left at the end of adolescence. [94]

A big reason people fail to get organized is laziness. We are all lazy in some areas of our lives. We need to identify those areas and then go to work to overcome them. We make ourselves do those things that we don't want to do. We make ourselves put the tools back when we are finished with them. We don't wait until tomorrow or next week. We do it now. Lazy people, however, don't complete what they began or even take advantage of the great opportunities in front of them: *"The lazy man does not roast what he took in hunting, but diligence is man's precious possession"* (Proverbs 12:27).

People judge our integrity by our level of organization. If we reply quickly to a request, people are impressed. If we fail to reply or are slow at it, we're considered sloppy and unreliable. If we're late for an appointment, the same conclusions are reached. People interpret tardiness as a character flaw or a lack of caring. You may think you're just disorganized, but those you're dealing with will see it as a problem of integrity.

DISCIPLINE

Whatever dreams we have will never be realized without discipline. The world lies at the feet of the disciplined person. A person's life lies wasted at the feet of indolence. Self-denial is the foundation of discipline. This is basic to the call of a Christian.

> *Then He said to them all, "If anyone desires to come after Me, let him deny himself, and take up his cross daily, and follow Me."* (Luke 9:23)

Oscar Wilde, the notably talented Irish-born writer most famous for the comedy *The Importance of Being Earnest,* lived a debauched lifestyle that eventually landed him in prison, where he spent the latter years of his life. Inside jail, he penned these words:

> The gods have given me almost everything, but I let myself be lured into long spells of senseless and sensual ease. Tired of being on the heights, I deliberately went to the depths in search of a new sensation. What paradox was to me in the sphere of thought, perversity became to me in the sphere of passion. I grew careless of the lives of others. I took pleasure where it pleased me, and passed on. I forgot that every little action of the common day makes or unmakes character, and that therefore what one has done in the secret chamber, one has some day to cry aloud from the housetop. I ceased to be lord over myself. I was no longer the captain of my soul, and I did not know it. I allowed pleasure to dominate me, and I ended in horrible disgrace. [95]

A poem Wilde wrote in prison reveals his deep remorse:

> And the wild regrets, and the bloody sweats,
> None knew so well as I,
> For he who lives more lives than one,
> More deaths than one must die. [96]

Discipline endures hardness, endures pain, and pays the price. Discipline keeps us in the harness when we don't want to stay there any longer. Discipline stops us from watching something on TV that we don't need to see but just want to. We do our work instead. Discipline keeps us in the producer zone rather than the consumer zone. We're creating, not consuming. We're doing, not talking. We're carrying, not being carried.

Discipline is sticking to the plan. A preacher I heard many years ago, an ex-army man named Hal Oxley, spoke of this matter in various ways. He said that the art of self-discipline enabled him to tell himself when he was going to sleep, and to sleep he would go! He spoke of infantrymen who needed to cross an area of barbed-wire fencing under gunfire. Because it would take too long to cut the wire, someone had to lay himself down on the wire and become a human bridge for the rest of the team. Generally, that soldier would die.

People judge our integrity by our level of organization.

Discipline means many things, including the highest of disciplines as disciples of Christ, when we are called to lay down our lives for one another. Hal also spoke of the means foot soldiers employed to defeat the charge of the cavalry. If the soldiers would join arms and stand, holding their position, the horses would inevitably balk at the last moment and throw their riders. The discipline required to hold still under such a threat is extraordinary. Ancient sailing ship captains would lash themselves to the pilot-wheels of their vessels in the midst of cyclonic storms and horrendous waves. This is what it means to have discipline in our lives—staying at the post, sticking to the job, doing whatever has to be done to accomplish the task.

fourteen

****

THE LEADER AND HIS TEAM

****

We don't just do business together; we live our lives with each other. That's how the team really gets in sync.

Probably the most crucial task we have as leaders is building a team. It is well documented, plainly obvious, and as sure as night follows day that a team accomplishes a thousand times more than we do on our own.

Moses clearly recognized this fact when he told his people that when they banded together, their capacity to defeat the enemy would multiply: *"Five of you shall chase a hundred, and a hundred of you shall put ten thousand to flight; your enemies shall fall by the sword before you"* (Leviticus 26:8).

One thing I am aware of is that without the incredible team of people I have around me, we could not achieve a minuscule portion of what we do. These people have proven themselves repeatedly to be those who are prepared to lay down their personal agendas for the accomplishment and health of the dream God has given us.

In our early days, we were faced with some tight financial pressures. My right-hand man and part of the original small team that started our church, Simon McIntyre, offered to forego his salary until we got through it. He has been called to serve alongside me and has played the most difficult instrument there is to play in the orchestra of any team—second fiddle. Often other ministers have asked him what his own vision is. His answer is, "I don't have one of those. My vision is to help Phil fulfill what God has given him to do." Today, Simon flies all over the world, preaching and teaching in a thousand different situations, enjoying blessing of all kinds, because he decided to be a team player and a great friend to me.

As sure as night follows day, a team accomplishes a thousand times more than we do on our own.

I've known men and women whom God has called to do the same in other teams, but they have failed to do so. Their ambitions have clouded their ability to perceive an honest opinion of their calling and abilities. They are not prepared to serve another, failing to realize that all leadership is based on servanthood. If we cannot love and serve a person we see, how can we love and serve God whom we cannot see? (See 1 John 4:20.) Some just have to have their own thing and be "the boss." I grieve for the people who have become kings of their own tiny fiefdoms when they could have been princes in vast kingdoms.

No longer do I call you servants, for a servant does not know what his master is doing; but I have called you friends, for all things that I heard from My Father I have made known to you. (John 15:15)

Greg French oversees the pastoral area of our church, providing for the nurturing of our people. He is involved in developing all kinds of leaders throughout our congregation. He is also a great team player, servant, and friend. He often travels with me, carrying bags and making all kinds of arrangements for the trip. Beyond these things, just being there for each other is what a team is all about. Greg will simply wait with me before I'm due to speak, either praying or standing nearby. There is strength in this for me, just knowing that there is someone else there. Playing an effective part in any team begins and ends with the fact that we care for one another.

These team relationships have not been developed in classrooms or in formal settings. These relationships take place when we "hang out" together, go on vacation together, or spend evenings out together with our wives. Basically, we don't just do business together; we live our lives with each other. That's how the team really gets in sync.

Because these relationships exist at the top of our organization, the sense of team, friendship, and servanthood to one another travels right through the entire church.

Great leaders never create politicking or intrigue among people and departments. They don't slander or libel others. They unite the organization rather than divide it. They support the whole. The team doesn't fragment, and team members work together. The overall goal is achieved.

The Importance of Team

In one of his Injoy Club audio tapes, John Maxwell tells the story of a horse-pulling contest in a small Midwestern town. The champion draft horse pulled 4,500 pounds, while the runner-up pulled 4,400 pounds. As a novelty, they yoked the two horses together to see what they could do. Amazingly, the team of draft horses pulled 12,500 pounds, which is one-third more than the sum of what they could pull individually. [97]

Great leaders never create politicking or intrigue; they unite the organization rather than divide it.

The folly of attempting to accomplish our tasks alone is highlighted in this explanation for an insurance claim by one hapless fellow:

Dear Sirs:

I am writing in response to your request for additional information in section 3 of the accident report form, which, as you know, asks for the cause of injuries. I had written, "Trying to do the job alone," and you asked for a fuller explanation. I trust that the following details will be sufficient:

I am a bricklayer by trade. On the day of the injuries, I was working alone. I had just completed laying bricks around the top of a six-story building when I realized that I had about five hundred pounds of bricks left over. Rather than carry the bricks down to ground level by hand, I decided to lower them in a barrel by using a rope and pulley, which was attached to the side of the building on the sixth floor. Securing the rope at ground level, I went up to the roof, swung the barrel out, and loaded the bricks into it.

Then I went back down and untied the rope, holding it tightly to ensure the slow descent of the 500-pound barrel of bricks. As you will note in section 11 of the accident report form, I weigh 160 pounds. Due to my shock at being jerked off the ground so swiftly, I lost my presence of mind for a moment and forgot to let go of the rope. Needless to say, I proceeded at a rapid rate up the side of the building. Somewhere between the second and third floors, I unfortunately met the barrel, which was proceeding downward at an equally impressive speed. This explains the chipped tooth, the broken collarbone, and the abrasions and bruises on my head and upper body, as listed in section 3 of the form.

Slowed only slightly, I continued my rapid ascent, not stopping until the fingers of my right hand were two knuckles deep into the pulley. This accounts for my broken thumb and index finger, as listed in section 3 of the report form.

Despite the pain, I retained my presence of mind and held tightly to the rope. However, at about the same time that my fingers were injured, the barrel hit the ground, and the bottom fell out of it, dumping the bricks in a big pile. Devoid of the bricks, the empty barrel weighed approximately 50 pounds. I refer you again to section 11 indicating my weight. As you can imagine, I began a rapid descent down the side of the building. In the vicinity of the third floor, I met the barrel coming up. This misfortune explains the fractured ankle and several lacerations on my legs and lower body, as reported in section 3 of the form.

At this point, the encounter with the barrel seemed to slow me down enough to lessen my injuries when I fell into the pile of bricks. Fortunately, only three vertebrae were cracked and the internal injuries were minimal, as indicated in section 3 of the form.

I am sorry to report, however, that as I lay there on the pile of bricks, in pain and unable to move, I again lost my composure and presence of mind, and let go of the rope. I could only lie there and watch the empty barrel begin its journey downward, plummeting the six stories to crash into me, which explains my two broken legs, as indicated in section 3 of the accident form.

While this appears to be a very involved explanation (it all happened in a matter of a few seconds), I trust this answers your concern. Please be assured that I am finished with trying to do the job alone.

Sincerely yours, [98]

Powerful dynamics happen when a team works together. Everyone achieves at higher levels. This means greater results for the team and for the individuals themselves. A team can achieve what is impossible for the solo player.

A team can achieve what is impossible for the solo player.

The apostle Paul defined a team and how it functions together in these terms:

For as the body is one and has many members, but all the members of that one body, being many, are one body, so also is Christ....But now God has set the members, each one of them, in the body just as He pleased....But now indeed there are many members, yet one body. And the eye cannot say to the hand, "I have no need of you"; nor again the head to the feet, "I have no need of you." No, much rather, those members of the body which seem to be weaker are necessary. And those members of the body which we think to be less honorable, on these we bestow greater honor; and our unpresentable parts have greater modesty, but our presentable parts have no need. But God composed the body, having given greater honor to that part which lacks it, that there should be no schism in the body, but that the members should have the same care for one another.

(1 Corinthians 12:12, 18, 20–25)

The purpose of God for our lives does not lie totally within ourselves. Much of it is actually in others. We don't have all the pieces for the jigsaw puzzle within ourselves. Many of the parts are in other people. This is why relationships are so important. The Devil attempts to divide us so that the plan of God remains unfulfilled. All of us have divine connections in our lives. Nurturing those relationships is important. We may not always find it easy relating to certain people, but God connects us together because there is a divine recipe in the mixture of certain personalities that achieves His plan.

Jonathan, the son of King Saul of Israel, knew that a major piece of the destiny for his life lay in his relationship with David. He prophesied to David, *"You shall be king over Israel, and I shall be next to you. Even my father Saul knows that"* (1 Samuel 23:17). But this cost him his relationship with his father. It was a choice he found too hard to make. He eventually died, headless, staked out on a Philistine wall next to his father (1 Samuel 31:10–12), never fulfilling the plan God had for his life.

Jesus applied this team principle to His disciples: *"And He called the twelve to Himself, and began to send them out two by two, and gave them power over unclean spirits"* (Mark 6:7). He knew His disciples would achieve much more working together than alone.

King Solomon listed the advantages of a team:

> *Two are better than one, because they have a good reward for their labor. For if they fall, one will lift up his companion. But woe to him who is alone when he falls, for he has no one to help him up. Again, if two lie down together, they will keep warm; but how can one be warm alone? Though one may be overpowered by another, two can withstand him. And a threefold cord is not quickly broken.* (Ecclesiastes 4:9–12)

According to Solomon,

❖ Teams have a greater reward for their work.

❖ Teams are able to support one another when they encounter trouble or if one actually falls. Two working together encourage one another.

❖ Teams are able to "warm" each other in times that are cold, lifting each others' spirits.

❖ Teams of two are more effective in battle than one and far more likely to succeed.

❖ Teams of three are even better in defeating the Enemy.

RELATIONAL SKILLS

No matter what the goal is about, relational skills are at a premium in maximizing the potential of the team's achievement of that goal. This is especially so in the church, where we rely on volunteers more than anyone or anything else for the work we do.

> **Teams are able to "warm" each other in times that are cold, lifting each others' spirits.**

Why will people work for nothing to fulfill the mission? Why will they do an excellent job? Why will they go the extra mile, give more time, and invest greater personal resources? Because their leaders understand relationships and the needs of individuals, as well as their prime motivators and reasons for being. Team leaders in churches understand what the primary call of Christ upon His church is, and they direct the workers to fulfill that call. The truth that the church is seeking to achieve God's desires will resonate in the spirit of every believer. If we as leaders have fires burning within to serve the Lord, the team will be drawn to the highest level of devotion for the task at hand.

ACCEPTANCE

Rejection is one of the worst experiences in life. Think through your own reactions to rejection: revenge, feelings of intense dislike, attitudes that dismiss "those people" as unimportant. Many people do not understand the power of acceptance and rejection. Taken to the extreme, rejection becomes prejudice and racism. Yet, in everyday life, in small as well as large contexts, acceptance and rejection still play their part.

Recently, I was about to board a flight out of Sydney. I went to the airline lounge of which I'm a member to wait until the plane was ready for boarding. The receptionist asked what flight I was on. It wasn't one of theirs, but that has happened before and has never been an issue. However, this person was determined to keep my wife and me out of the lounge because we were flying on a different carrier. I was embarrassed. Though this was only a small issue, I am still amazed at how quickly my attitude changed toward that person and the lounge, and then the entire airline. In no time I was saying, "This whole airline needs to get its act together." Then my negative attitude had spread to include the whole country: "What's this country coming to, fussing about what flights we're on!" And on and on....

Acceptance, on the other hand, is as powerful a force for the positive. We love those who accept us when they could reject us. If that attendant had said, "Well, the policy is such and such, but I'll let you in," I would have immediately felt accepted, and I wouldn't have even begun to think of flying with any other airline.

Whatever we have, we have so we can give it away.

We speak well of people who accept us. They, and what they represent, become the best in our eyes. When we include people in our world, they feel accepted. Inclusion and acceptance provide the environment in which the best qualities of others can flourish.

Whatever we have, we have so we can give it away. If we have position, we don't have it so we can exclude others. We have it so we can give it to others by including them in our world. How many times do we see people get introduced into the inner circle of leadership, only to watch them keep out anybody else trying to get in? Position has the potential of rendering people useless in terms of developing others. The very act of inclusion gives people something to live up to.

DELEGATION

You can't do it all. We're not called to do it all. In fact, there is holiness about remaining within the calling we have. At least twice in the Bible, we come across men who imagine they can simply carry out the task of another without any repercussions. Uzziah, an immensely successful king, had no difficulty in believing he could not only be the king of the nation, but also carry out priestly duties as well. The brave priests attempted to warn the presumptuous man of the consequences. He ignored them to his peril. He was smitten with leprosy and had it to the end of his days.

> *Then Uzziah became furious; and he had a censer in his hand to burn incense. And while he was angry with the priests, leprosy broke out on his forehead, before the priests in the house of the LORD, beside the incense altar.* (2 Chronicles 26:19)

Saul fell into the same trap of failing to remain within the calling upon his life. The priests were appointed by God for the presenting of sacrifices. They always made an offering to God before they engaged in warfare. However, according to Saul, the man ordained for the job of priest, Samuel, was taking too long to come and make the sacrifice before the Israelite army went into battle, and so he took the responsibility upon himself. Saul had grown impatient. He wanted to get on with the business of war. God did not treat this matter lightly. Saul eventually lost his kingdom, and this brazen act of assuming the responsibilities and calling of another leader contributed heavily to Saul's downfall. (See 1 Samuel 13:8–14.)

Teams begin with discipling, which is delegation in management terminology. Leaders have a wonderful ability to give people jobs that they love to do. The leader's greatest achievement is to get thousands of people doing something they would never have done otherwise, have them enjoy doing it, and succeed in the effort.

There are four reasons we fail to delegate:

1. We don't believe anyone else can do it as well as we can.

2. We don't want anyone else to do it. We enjoy doing it too much.

3. We don't trust anyone else to do it. Our emotional ceiling prevents us from delegating responsibilities. It involves too much trust in others and produces too much anxiety in us. Increasing our own faith, training others, and requiring higher levels of accountability will lift the ceiling.

4. We fear someone else may do it better and thus make us look bad.

Teams begin with discipling, which is delegation in management terms.

I have had associates who find it almost impossible to relinquish areas of their churches that others could easily be taking care of, such as new Christian classes, new members classes, Bible college oversight, and so on. For the church to grow, these areas need to be delegated to others. If they're not, the church will be stunted in its growth. Why? No minister can cope with doing it all.

The incredible thing is that others will not only do the job well, but they will often do it better.

One Sunday, we were holding one of our regular baptismal services down at the beach in a large rock pool. I was tired and trying to get through the list of people to be baptized reasonably quickly. I had already preached a couple of times that morning and had another service shortly. As I was standing there, I realized my mind wasn't really on the job. I didn't have the enthusiasm I should have had, so I asked a couple of the small group leaders standing nearby to come and finish baptizing. They couldn't believe it. "Us?!" As they baptized the rest of the people, they prayed the power of God over them with fiery prayers and prophetic words. They conducted one of the best baptismal services I've ever witnessed.

fifteen

THE LEADER'S TEAM
IN SCRIPTURE

A s we saw in the last chapter, delegation is an important part of leadership. In fact, the Bible holds many examples of delegation, from which we can learn important leadership principles.

FIVE GREAT MOMENTS OF DELEGATION

1. FOR PASTORING

The following passage provides extraordinary insight into the development of the leadership team over the newly formed Israelite nation:

And so it was, on the next day, that Moses sat to judge the people; and the people stood before Moses from morning until evening. So when Moses' father-in-law saw all that he did for the people, he said, "What is this thing that you are doing for the people? Why do you alone sit, and all the people stand before you from morning until evening?" And Moses said to his father-in-law, "Because the people come to me to inquire of God. When they have a difficulty, they come to me, and I judge between one and another; and I make known the statutes of God and His laws." So Moses' father-in-law said to him, "The thing that you do is not good. Both you and these people who are with you will surely wear yourselves out. For this thing is too much for you; you are not able to perform it by yourself. Listen now to my voice; I will give you counsel, and God will be with you: Stand before God for the people, so that you may bring the difficulties to God. And you shall teach them the statutes and the laws, and show them the way in which they must walk and the work they must do. Moreover you shall select from all the people able men, such as fear God, men of truth, hating covetousness; and place such over them to be rulers of thousands, rulers of hundreds, rulers of fifties, and rulers of tens. And let them judge the people at all times. Then it will be that every great matter they shall bring to you, but every small matter they themselves shall judge. So it will be easier for you, for they will bear the burden with you. If you do this thing, and God so commands you, then you will be able to endure, and all this people will also go to their place in peace." So Moses heeded the voice of his father-in-law and did all that he had said. (Exodus 18:13–24)

There are some salient points we can learn from this passage, which provides background for the counsel of Jethro to Moses.

❖ It may be flattering to have people stand before you from morning until evening; however, that is not the will of God.

❖ Moses thought he was the only one who could hear from God.

❖ Some things that we think we do well might actually be substandard. If we assume more responsibility than we are called to, we will not last. The work in itself may be good, but the fact that we're doing it is not.

❖ If we're wearing out and our people are, too, we're doing something wrong. When burnout is common, something is wrong.

If we assume more responsibility than we are called to, we will not last.

❖ Listening to wise counsel brings God's presence in our lives. The reverse is also true. When we refuse wise counsel, God will not be with us. Moses had every reason not to listen. The man had split the Red Sea. He had destroyed the economy, agriculture, and health of one of the most powerful nations in the world. He had destroyed the entire Egyptian army. All this he had done single-handedly, but he was still meek enough to hear the counsel of his father-in-law, Jethro, who was just a farmer, running a little village. Jethro lived a godly life, but his accomplishments certainly didn't match those of Moses; Jethro had earned the respect of Moses, and he had the wisdom to guide the new leader.

❖ Jethro established the first priority in Moses' life—to stand before God for the people, with their problems, and pray for them. Prayer was his first calling. The next was to teach the Word.

❖ Moses was called and gifted to teach the people the ways of God—how to walk and how to work. People are in our care to work, not just observe. We imagine people know instinctively how to walk, but we all need teaching in how to live as Christians. We need inspiration and instruction to live for God.

❖ From day one, our people should be given tasks. People who sit, sour. People who work, grow. Sometimes people may complain, but that is no reason for them to stop working. The complaint of a working person is far preferable to the criticism of the idle.

❖ Moses delegated according to capability. We must know our people. Some can lead ten, some a hundred, and some a thousand.

In the realm of church leadership, one reason the pastor of a church resists delegating the work of shepherding to others is because of the traditional notion that the pastor of a church is the boss. If we ask, "Who's the pastor around here?" we generally mean, "Who's the boss?" However, that's not always the case. The original leader of the church at Ephesus was the apostle Paul, who was succeeded by Priscilla and Aquilla (Acts 18:19), who were succeeded by the pastor Timothy (1 Timothy 1:3). Tradition has it that the apostle John cared for the church in the later years of his life.

The leader of a church need not necessarily be the pastor. Many of those called to lead churches today attempt to be pastors when, in fact, that is not their primary calling. Traditional expectations bind a person to a life of frustration while they try to be someone that they are not. This does not mean the leader has no concern for the flock. Leaders will always have shepherds' hearts, but they must be able to turn the pastoral responsibilities of the church over to other people gifted for that task and devote themselves to what they're primarily called to.

The leader of a church need not necessarily be the pastor.

2. FOR WAR

The second great moment of delegation in Scripture was when war broke out against Israel on her journey from Egypt to the Promised Land. Under attack from Amalek, Moses told Joshua to select men who would go out, and to fight for them.

> *And Moses said to Joshua, "Choose us some men and go out, fight with Amalek. Tomorrow I will stand on the top of the hill with the rod of God in my hand."*
>
> (Exodus 17:9)

Moses trusted Joshua to select a team responsible for victory on behalf of the entire nation. A key man like Joshua selected others without much reference to the leader. Moses chose the position of prayer for himself.

This was a difficult choice. Moses had been trained in the Egyptian courts in the art of war (Acts 7:22). Josephus described his military successes and exploits, especially against the Ethiopians, this way:

Moses then achieved his march and defeated the Ethiopians in a surprise attack. They fled Egypt, and were pursued by Moses into their own country and defeated again, to the extent they were in danger of being reduced to slavery. [99]

Moses knew how to wage war, and wage it successfully, yet this was not his calling at that time. His part was to stand before God for the people. Joshua was the man for the war.

Similarly, the apostles were asked to solve a prejudice problem in the early church. They refused, saying they were needed instead for prayer and the Word (Acts 6:2–4). They held to the priority for their lives. They began team building. They appointed men held in respect by the people to attend to the problem, which was capably solved.

Delegating tasks to others requires greater levels of trust than we have previously placed in people. However, without crossing that barrier, we remain severely limited. For our churches to grow, we must personally grow. Handing over conflict for others to resolve requires us to develop greater trust, both in God and in the people handling it.

The first church Chris and I pastored was in Lyttelton, New Zealand. It's a small church in a very small town. In the three years we were there, the church grew astronomically, from 15 people to 35! God worked in me, developing, changing, and hammering my life into some useable form for the future. While I was there, I learned some tough lessons in a very limited environment. Thankfully, the damage to others and my embarrassment were both contained by the smallness of our world during that time.

One of the most powerful lessons I learned in our little church in Lyttelton was in the realm of delegation. When we started the church, I was doing everything. On Sundays I set the chairs out, greeted the people, played the guitar, led the singing, took the offering, gave the announcements, preached the message, prayed for the people, shook their hands as they left, put away the chairs, and went home. The Lord told me very clearly one day to ask a young girl in the church to play the guitar. I had heard her play the instrument and was not that impressed. I resisted. Yet the anointing for worship leading was not on me anymore, and I knew it.

For our churches to grow, we must personally grow.

I gave the guitar to the girl for one song. I didn't think the music was that great, but the people were lost in worship. She didn't know the next song very well, so I took the guitar back. The anointing lifted again. I could hear myself singing. I was completely self-conscious. Nobody was worshipping. Amazing! I asked Melva to lead again, and the anointing returned. Slowly I began learning to give things away.

The years passed, and we arrived in Sydney. This time we had genuinely seen incredible growth in our church. I was feeling that I had learned the art of delegation reasonably well—that is, until one day when I was faced with several serious conflicts, the likes of which I had never encountered before.

As a general principle in my life, I make lists of everything—problems, faults, tasks—everything. During this time I had a list of 32 problems. Five of them were within our own church. The others were outside our church. They all ranged from "quite serious" to "really serious."

The worst was that a terrible tragedy had taken place, and a woman had died. As a missionary to the Philippines, she had been raped and murdered while attempting to minister to inmates in a prison. She had attended one of our churches at one time, and her parents were upset, thinking we had sent her out inadequately prepared, even though she had gone of her own volition some time after having left the church.

It was obviously a very grievous time for the family as they tried to understand why this had happened. Anyway, it made national television news, and I was on talk shows and various other news media trying to "handle" the situation. Moreover, I had four other situations at this level of intensity happening at the same time. I felt like I was drowning, trying to handle them all.

I was feeling completely besieged when the Lord spoke to me clearly. He told me to delegate conflict. I was thinking that I had given away just about everything I could. I honestly felt there was no one else who could take on these highly sensitive situations and get satisfactory answers, especially when it came to dealing with the media. The future perception of our church in the community hung on the outcome. It seemed to me that any one of these disasters could bury us. Finally, with a lot of hesitation, I asked my two right-hand men to handle one of the situations. They went to work and, to my amazement, resolved the problem. With the situation settled, I realized my faith in those around me needed to grow.

Moses delegated the conflict with the Amalekites into the hands of Joshua. He ascended the mountain with the clear realization that everyone has a particular calling and place in God and His church. We must know what our particular calling is and do it. We cannot play every position on the field. The church acts as one body. Every member is called to a particular function. When members are active in their calling, the church grows.

From whom the whole body, joined and knit together by what every joint supplies, according to the effective working by which every part does its share, causes growth of the body for the edifying of itself in love.

(Ephesians 4:16)

The team members we choose need to be able to fight for us and for our vision.

The team members we choose need to be able to fight for us and for our vision. The people we choose must have the ability to fight and win. They need to have proven themselves in spiritual battles, and they need to have triumphed. They need to be overcomers. They need to display consistently positive attitudes. These people do not just attend, support, or watch, but they must fight—for us! They shouldn't fight only for their own victories. They need to fight for the church. They need to defend the pastor when he's criticized and fight for the church's reputation, spiritual health, and finances. They need to be genuine soldiers for God.

We have a program in our church called Connect Now. Within this program are eight initiatives that are designed to reach the unchurched for Christ. One of those initiatives is contacting people who were previously members of our church and have slipped away. I so admire the people involved in this outreach because they hear all the worst criticisms about the pastor, about the church, and about what we do, yet they keep reaching out to these people and eventually win them back to the Lord.

These people have to be soldiers. They can't be involved in the conversation, listening to all the gripes of these people (which often sound very plausible), and get swung over to the negative side. This is a war in which misperceptions are deposited in people's minds by the Devil. Those involved in dismantling them must be tough enough to "fight for us."

When we're in the trenches getting fired at, I don't want soldiers at my side wondering why their leader is being fired upon. People like this can eventually turn their guns on their leader. They imagine the Enemy must have good reason for shooting at their leader, and so they begin firing also.

Once we've been in the trenches a few times, we realize who can be trusted under fire. Even if the leader does make a mistake, that is still no reason for those around him or her to attack. I want to know that my team will be loyal to me when the attacks are unjustified and even when they are justified. I don't expect to live my life without making mistakes. I want them to help me get through whatever the mistake is so we can get to the end of this calling together.

For far too long, however, the church has shot its wounded. We've got to heal fallen soldiers. I have learned that if I give mercy, my people will return it when I need it. I've seen pastors who are hard and merciless on their people. Then when they make mistakes—which is inevitable—mercy simply isn't there for them because they have never modeled it themselves. It's not a part of the culture.

The selection of the right people is paramount to enjoying great fruitfulness as a team. The most common challenge for leaders is finding capable assistants. All the ministries in our churches, from youth leaders to music directors to associate pastors, are best "homegrown." Abraham trained those who were born *"in his own house"* (Genesis 14:14) to be an extremely effective band of soldiers. Church growth and development depends on the continual development and release of new ministers into the church. Those people God gives us are rarely trained when they come. This is so that we can place our particular anointing and environmental culture into their lives. They come unprepared so that we can go to work at making them ready.

**Once we've been in the trenches a few times,
we realize who can be trusted under fire.**

Most often the people we seek are right under our noses. Our problem is actually not a lack of people. People can become anything under the right conditions. Anything is possible. It is not dependent upon how we have been raised, what star we were born under, what sort of events made up our childhood, or whether we're gifted or not.

If a person has a right attitude, everything is possible, and nothing is impossible. Our problem, in not having the right kind of people, is within us. We will only fail to develop people within our own ranks if we fail to believe that those we have are up to the task.

The simple act of believing in a person yields an amazing amount of accomplishment. All that most people need is for someone to believe in them. This releases a river of potential. As we trust people with assignments, they rise to levels of accomplishment that surprise even the cynics. We think that it's a matter of education, experience, contacts, or talent. All these are obviously valuable, but ultimately it's a matter of faith, the faith of someone who believes in us. Leaders are developed not in classrooms, but on the job.

Apprentice-style training reaps the greatest rewards. C. Peter Wagner notes that individuals who have not had formal training but have been developed in apprenticeship situations lead all the largest and fastest-growing churches of South America. They have been in harness with another leader of God, doing His business, not just learning about it.

If a person has a right attitude, everything is possible, and nothing is impossible.

We may think that the tasks are beyond the people we have around us. However, unless people are stretched, they will never rise to their full potential. Just the act of giving someone a task more demanding than what they've attempted before reveals that you believe they are capable. This, in itself, motivates a person to higher levels of accomplishment.

Nancy Dornan said, "When you believe in people, they do the impossible."[100] We mistakenly believe that someone else from somewhere else will do better than anyone we have in our own ranks.

Abraham's method of developing leaders from within was far preferable to getting someone from elsewhere. If people do come from outside, give them time to be "baptized" into the church so they share the vision like everybody else. To become true sons and daughters of the church, they need to drink the milk (accept the teaching), imbibe the spirit (accept the attitude of the church), and take on the name (be proud of belonging to the congregation).

People must have certain character traits before they are commissioned. Competency shouldn't be at the top of the list. No, that's not a typo. Competency is not at the top of the list. If people are already competent at what they do, then they are not challenged to grow. It's simply a job that both they and you know they can do.

Discipleship is delegation, plus teaching, plus training, plus deploying. The process of delegation is discipleship. Jesus has called us to make disciples (Matthew 28:19). This is not only teaching others, but also causing them to actually do what Jesus taught. Without delegation, churches cannot grow.

Hindrances to delegation can be emotional, psychological, or spiritual. Ministers are often unable to let go of certain areas of their leadership. We also have problems with the concept of others doing what we have been doing. Often, we simply fail to impart the mantle that will equip the person with supernatural abilities for the job.

3. FOR OVERSIGHT

So Moses said to the LORD, "Why have You afflicted Your servant? And why have I not found favor in Your sight, that You have laid the burden of all these people on me? Did I conceive all these people? Did I beget them, that You should say to me, 'Carry them in your bosom, as a guardian carries a nursing child,' to the land which You swore to their fathers? Where am I to get meat to give to all these people? For they weep all over me, saying, 'Give us meat, that we may eat.' I am not able to bear all these people alone, because the burden is too heavy for me." (Numbers 11:11–14)

Moses found that bearing the burden of the newly set-free Israelites was too much to bear. They were weeping and complaining because they had no meat, only the manna they collected each morning.

Discipleship is delegation, plus teaching, plus training, plus deploying.

Moses loved them, but that was the problem. They were a painful people to lead. Carrying a love for them in his heart was the burden. Yet they were grieving both him and God. Moses felt completely inadequate for the task. God's answer was delegation. He responded to Moses, not by telling him that if the job was too much, then he no longer had the job; rather, God directed Moses to distribute the burden among seventy other leaders. Moses was instructed to gather the elders at the tabernacle so the Lord could anoint them.

Then I will come down and talk with you there. I will take of the Spirit that is upon you and will put the same upon them; and they shall bear the burden of the people with you, that you may not bear it yourself alone. (Numbers 11:17)

This clearly shows that the capacity to guide God's people is a gift from God. It is not just about leadership skills. It's about anointing. Moses had received an anointing for the task of delivering and leading the nation God had formed. However, the stress this placed on him proved to be too great on a sustained basis. The only answer was to share the load.

Note that it took seventy men to carry the burden Moses had been shouldering alone. Too often, too many ministers feel this high stress level, yet they fail to delegate, resulting in breakdowns of all kinds. Dr. David Yonggi Cho tells of the early days in his church when he was doing everything. He ran his church like this for a number of years until he learned the lesson of delegation in a painful way. On one particular Sunday after preaching in two services, he held a baptismal service for around three hundred people. After that, he interpreted for another preacher, and toward the end of the message, he suffered a complete nervous breakdown. It took him a decade to recover. "For the next ten years, from 1964 to 1974, I felt as though I was dying every minute." [101] For a few years, he could only preach for around ten minutes before he would collapse again.

While Dr. Cho was hospitalized, he felt the Lord leading him to delegate the responsibility of pastoring the church to the people in small groups. He then developed the cell group system, which has proven to be so successful in his church.

At first, he was very concerned whether or not it would work. One of the main challenges was that most of the available leaders were women, because the men worked for such long hours. The status of women as leaders was not highly regarded in the church culture. This was a revolutionary move. However, he persisted and found the women doing just as effective work as the men.

Since then, small home groups have proven to be one of the most successful building blocks for church growth in the history of Christendom, but what a drastic way to discover delegation! Many of us could prevent disasters to our health, families, and ministries if we would simply be prepared to share the burden of the call with others.

4. For Ministry Empowerment

And when He had called His twelve disciples to Him, He gave them power over unclean spirits, to cast them out, and to heal all kinds of sickness and all kinds of disease. (Matthew 10:1)

This was an amazing moment in the life of the disciples. Immediately prior to this, Jesus was lamenting the fact that a vast harvest was ready to be reaped, but there were few reapers. He saw hungry and thirsty people everywhere, yet the capacity to meet the need was too small when it was limited to just one person, even when that person was Jesus Himself.

However, Jesus had compassion on the great multitude of people flocking to Him (v. 36). They were weary and scattered, like sheep without a shepherd. This stirred His compassion.

There could not be a better description of the state of the people of the world today. Stress is at an all-time high. Once upon a time, the advertisements for vacations described big parties and long nights we could anticipate; the tours here, there, and everywhere we could hope for. Nowadays, it's the long deserted beach where no one else will bother us, filled with quiet, do-nothing days. People are weary and scattered.

Today, we live in one of the most transient societies in history. Instead of living in the same family home for our whole life, we live in a series of different homes. Instead of just one marriage partner, it is estimated that throughout the average person's lifetime they will have two to three marriage partners. Instead of living in just one town or country, people move around from place to place at an ever-increasing rate. Although this certainly increases career opportunities and expands the life experience, it also develops an uneasy sense of rootlessness and lack of belonging.

Many of us could prevent disasters if we would simply be prepared to share the burden of the call with others.

The other aspect of this scatteredness is the desperate need people have to understand where they are meant to be going and what they are meant to be doing with their lives. We have become enmeshed in a psychic society trying to decipher the mysteries of guidance for our lives.

Just as it did in New Testament days, this scatteredness elicits the compassion of Jesus today. His answer is to empower His disciples to do exactly what He is doing. He calls His disciples to Himself. He doesn't call the multitude who are hopeful of the miracles for this task. He doesn't call the seventy to whom He has given the work of preparation. He calls His disciples, those more interested in Him than in anything else. He calls those who are considered disciples, people living by principle and not just emotion, those who are ready to go all the way with the Lord, those who are friends of God.

The first step in empowerment from Christ is to respond to His call to Himself. The primary call upon every believer and minister is not to the ministry, but to Jesus Christ Himself. We have nothing to offer people if we do not have the Lord.

We read of the journey into relationship with the Lord in Psalm 23. David first spoke of *"the Lord"* as his shepherd. This is a statement about Yahweh, a theological statement about God's role in our lives. However, David progressed to addressing the Lord as *"He"*—the recognition of God as a person rather than just an impersonal force—when he wrote of God leading him, feeding him, bringing him to rest, and restoring his soul.

Yet David's hunger for closeness was still not satisfied. He continued to move closer to the Lord, regarding Him as a person he was in a direct, face-to-face relationship with. As David traveled through the valley, he drew closest to the Lord. It's as if he turned his head and faced God Almighty as his Friend and said, *"Though I walk through the valley of the shadow of death,...You are with me"* (v. 4).

We come to the Lord as disciples. He empowers us to cast out demons and to heal all kinds of diseases. I have no doubt that Jesus laid hands on the disciples to impart this power. This is a normal mode of impartation throughout Scripture. Moses laid hands upon Joshua, giving him the same anointing of wisdom that he had.

Now Joshua the son of Nun was full of the spirit of wisdom, for Moses had laid his hands on him; so the

children of Israel heeded him, and did as the LORD had
commanded Moses. (Deuteronomy 34:9)

Jacob used the laying on of hands to impart blessing on his children (Genesis 48:14). The apostles employed the laying on of hands in the early church (Acts 6:6), as did Paul in praying for Timothy (1 Timothy 4:14 and 5:22).

The interesting point here is that after Jesus had given them this power, the Scripture says, *"Now, the names of the twelve apostles are..."* (Matthew 10:2). They came as disciples and were empowered. They left as apostles. These men turned the world upside down.

The first step in empowerment from Christ is to respond to His call to Himself.

As we welcome men and women who have been called of God to work with us, we are able to impart to them power for serving God in the same manner as ourselves. Some of us have attempted to impart this power for the ministry work to others, but have found our attempts ineffective. Our capacity to impart the anointing rests in the fact that we want impartation to happen and in our determination to impart to others. If we are fearful of others having what we have, we will never really impart that same power and anointing God has placed upon us.

5. FOR PROBLEM SOLVING

In the first five chapters of the book of Acts, it is obvious that the early church enjoyed amazing success. People were being added to the church daily. In an atmosphere of enormous joy, powerful prayers and amazing miracles were taking place every day.

There was also a high level of negative reaction. Some of the best leaders were thrown into prison, and a tide of persecution had begun to rise.

The church, in a progressive revelation of its identity, steadily increased in its understanding of who its members were as followers of Jesus, going from "souls" to "believers" to "disciples."

Our capacity to impart the anointing rests in the fact that we want impartation to happen.

This corresponded to a progressively increasing growth rate in the church. At first when the new Christians were referred to as *"souls"* and the church as *"them,"* we are told that people were *"added"* to their number (Acts 2:41). However, as they grew in the knowledge of who they were individually, and as the Christians were referred to as *"believers"* and *"the church,"* they were *"increasingly added"* to the kingdom (Acts 5:14). Yet as they entered into a lifestyle of discipleship and were referred to as *"disciples,"* we are told that they began to "multiply" (Acts 6:1). Any of us with even the slightest knowledge of mathematics can understand that multiplying increases numbers a lot faster than simply adding.

In Acts 6, a situation emerged that the church had never encountered before. Suddenly they were faced not with problems from without, but from within. And it was not a small problem. Complaints were brought to the apostles that the Hellenistic-speaking widows were being discriminated against.

Part of the mission of the early church was to care for its widows. Every day, distribution was made to these needy women. However, the purist Hebrews were keeping the provisions back from those women they considered as not being a part of the pure Jewish bloodline. This had all the potential to escalate into a terrible division in the young fledgling church.

The problem was brought to the apostles. Surprisingly, their response was far from anxious. They declared that their first priority was to attend to the Word of God and prayer, not to the managing or solving of these sorts of problems.

I find this an amazing decision. They could have been accused of being uncaring and disinterested in the social justice of even their own church. Widows were among the most vulnerable group of people on earth, people with no means of support.

The apostles were not uncaring, though; they told the church to select *"seven men of good reputation, full of the Holy Spirit and wisdom"* (Acts 6:3). Once these men were chosen, the apostles laid hands on them, and these men not only sorted out the problem, but were also powerfully used by God to bring about revival in the early church. The most amazing thing about this is that, directly after the apostles had delegated authority and ministry to these men, the church did not just multiply; rather it *"multiplied greatly"* (v. 7).

This is the optimum growth level for the church. It is too often missed because pastors are more involved in management than they are in their primary calling, which is the

Word of God and prayer. While we are distracted from doing what only we can do, we are most often doing things others could do. And while we are doing those things, nobody else is exercising their ministry in that area, or at least learning to.

If the church is to start moving in a greater growth mode, we must begin delegating the thousands of tasks that steal us from our primary calling for God.

Paul's instruction to Timothy was the wise Master Builder's wisdom for the management of the house of God: "Give the ministry away to others."

> *And the things that you have heard from me among many witnesses, commit these to faithful men who will be able to teach others also.* (2 Timothy 2:2)

sixteen

WHO'S ON THE TEAM?

There are factors that either qualify or disqualify people from being part of our dreams and therefore part of our teams. Many people want to be in ministry, but not all will be. The standard should always be kept high so that a precedent exists for others to emulate. We are tempted to compromise our standards for the sake of getting someone who "at least can do the job."

Training a person for a job is easy compared to changing a person's character and attitudes. These are far deeper areas that take time and testing to develop. Good leaders don't become so desperate that they compromise on these areas. Many times we have selected people with less natural skills than others, who would be a more obvious addition to the team except that their immaturity in Christ eclipsed their competency.

The funny thing about only settling for the best is that you will usually get it. God equips people with abilities beyond their training if their hearts are right toward Him.

Moses and David both become architects and designers because of visions that God gave them. Neither of them was trained in this area, yet they designed some of the greatest buildings in history.

MAKING THE RIGHT SELECTION

What follows are key qualities that you should look for in potential team members. Remember, a team is only as good as its members, and members are only as good as their character. Make sure you make the right selection by picking quality team members.

FAITHFULNESS

Faithfulness encompasses three primary character qualities:

* *Regularity.* People must be predictable and regular. "Thereness" is essential. People with unstable living patterns can't be relied upon to be available when you need them.

* *Trueness of spirit.* They must be privately honorable, not just publicly upright. Authenticity rings clear in their expressions.

* *Loyalty to the leadership and the church.* Loyalty is under challenge when opportunities for criticism are high. Loyalty is not only expressed in passive non-criticism or in "support" of the church and its leadership; rather, those people who are part of the team must fight for the church and its leaders. Their concern manifests itself in practical, self-sacrificing ways.

Proven faithfulness requires time. Time reveals people as they are. Jesus identified faithfulness in three areas.

FAITHFULNESS IN LITTLE THINGS

He who is faithful in what is least is faithful also in much; and he who is unjust in what is least is unjust also in much. (Luke 16:10)

Attention to detail is vital. Overlooking tiny issues because they are small and insignificant reveals motives that are not true. Faithfulness is being concerned with the *"least"* things. Large doors swing on little hinges.

A team is only as good as its members, and members are only as good as their character.

In September 1620, the Pilgrims left Plymouth, England, for America aboard the Mayflower. In November, they reached Provincetown Harbor, near Cape Cod, Massachusetts. Pilgrim leaders wrote and signed The Mayflower Compact, forming the first American constitutional democracy. They settled on the site of what is now Plymouth, Massachusetts. The Plymouth settlers held a dream for an America under God. This vast vision began with the smallest group of people arriving on the shores of the new land.

> Thus out of small beginnings greater things have been produced by His hand that made all things of nothing, and gives being to all things that are; and, as one small candle may light a thousand, so the light here kindled hath shone unto many, yea in some sort to our whole nation.[102]

281

The prophet Zechariah asked us not to despise the day of small beginnings (Zechariah 4:10).

The entire kingdom of God is based on the seed principle, as is the entire natural kingdom. Everything begins from the smallest of beginnings. If we fail to give due attention to the seed, we will never reap the harvest destined for our lives.

FAITHFULNESS WITH MONEY

Therefore if you have not been faithful in the unrighteous mammon, who will commit to your trust the true riches? (Luke 16:11)

Faithfulness with money proves a person can handle spiritual riches. I find it easy to think this is the wrong way around. Surely if a person is first spiritually faithful, God will then entrust him or her with finances. Not so! God watches the way we pay our bills, spend our money, arrange priorities, and how we generate and handle money. He figures whether or not we are faithful on this basis.

It amazes me how many Christians think they can skirt the law because they are believers. They approach business in a very shabby manner and expect to prosper. This will never happen. When I was witnessing to a wealthy young man recently, he told me most Christians he had dealt with were crooked. He's a real estate agent, and he had come across several Christians who hadn't paid their rent. They had also told lies about their previous financial situations so they could be approved to rent a house, taken too long to pay commissions, or tried to get out of that part of the sale of their house completely.

Christians have become notorious for trying to get freebies. This is a bad testimony. Christians must behave properly in the business world. Generosity, honesty, and integrity should all be hallmarks of believers' dealings in this world.

Much of this practice comes out of a poverty mentality. Because many Christians think it is pious to be poor, they are left with having to expect some kind of charity to come their way to make up for their lack.

Faithfulness with money proves a person can handle spiritual riches.

The fact of the matter is that people end up serving money more out of the lack of it than out of an abundance of it. The way it influences people to act is wrong. I've known believers to justify not leaving a tip for waiters and waitresses. Instead, they leave tracts about the Lord. This is terrible! A far better witness would be a generous tip. The fact that a tract is left instead of a tip just confirms the average unbeliever's dismal view of stingy Christians and certainly reinforces a poor impression of Christianity.

FAITHFULNESS WITH OTHER PEOPLE'S PROPERTY

And if you have not been faithful in what is another man's, who will give you what is your own? (Luke 16:12)

Faithfulness with others' property qualifies a person for selection in God's work. The real point is that the entire life of a minister is spent in caring for the lives of others. If he is caring for his own life at the expense of others, this will show in the way he handles other people's money, dreams, family, and so on.

When King David and his army returned from defeating the Amalekites who had burned Ziklag, David's stronghold, he had recovered all the Amalekites had taken from them—both their families and possessions. Certain soldiers had remained to guard the supplies, and David rewarded them with exactly the same reward as those who went to the battle (1 Samuel 30:24). As far as God is concerned, caring for the property and interests of others is a high indication of faithfulness.

People who work hard to fulfill the dreams of another find their own dreams coming to pass. Joseph spent his life interpreting the dreams of others. He interpreted the baker's dreams and the butler's dream. He then interpreted the king's dream. Because he did this, his own dream came to pass. The overwhelming purpose of the servant of God is to interpret the dream of the Father in heaven: *"Thy will be done"* (Matthew 6:10, KJV). Faithfulness is gauged by the way we handle the dreams and visions of our pastors, our families, our children, our spouses, our friends, and our churches.

CONSECRATION TO GOD

Potential team members must sacrifice their lives to God. This is displayed in their devotion to the local church. Jesus loves His church. Anyone wanting to serve Him in His house must love the church as well.

Consecration to God is revealed by the fact that they keep their lives clean and undefiled from the world. These people are separated to God and whatever He wants them to do.

If we are failing to produce at least some people like this under our ministry, something is wrong, because these are the qualities of normal discipleship. We need to redefine our ministry, understand exactly what God has called us to do, and apply ourselves fully to that end.

No matter what we say, we only ever reproduce what we are.

People who work hard to fulfill the dreams of another find their own dreams coming to pass.

TEACHABILITY

If people are unable to be taught, to receive teaching, or to implement counsel in their lives, they are basically useless for the work of God. Until this quality is in our lives, we have no capacity to grow and change. Without teachable spirits, we are unable to acquire the skills God gives for His work.

Do you see a man wise in his own eyes? There is more hope for a fool than for him.　　(Proverbs 26:12)

In today's world, I have found it increasingly difficult to actually speak into people's lives. The belief in individual independence is increasing in society. Yet people who are not just open to instruction, but are actually eager to be coached in life, are the ones who receive guidance even when it is not being intentionally given. They create an environment in which discipling people is simple. A wise person actually draws counsel out of mentors.

Counsel in the heart of man is like deep water, but a man of understanding will draw it out.　　(Proverbs 20:5)

TRUSTWORTHINESS

But let these also first be tested; then let them serve as deacons, being found blameless.　　(1 Timothy 3:10)

****

"Tested." This means that we have given people small jobs, and they have executed them well enough to be trusted with something larger. They have proven themselves.

It also means that they have overcome temptations and emerged victorious from difficult times in their personal world. This is the most general meaning of the word *"tested"* in Scripture.

===

If people are unable to be taught, they are basically useless for the work of God.

****

They have the basics of the Christian life well under control. Attending church is a number one priority for these people. They have a passion for the house of God. They have the disciplines of daily prayer and Bible reading. Their family life is in good order. Their morals, ethics, and attitudes are unquestionable.

Don't settle for less. Talent is no substitute for the qualities of a committed Christian who is filled with the Holy Spirit.

Proven people have submissive, teachable, cooperative, non-critical attitudes. Without these qualities, people disqualify themselves from being chosen for effective service. Once people have developed these traits, they become effective for God.

Character, integrity, and ethics are intact and unquestionable in a true leader. This is what the church is built on—not on talent, style, personality, or skill, which all take second place to the godliness of a person's life.

Some circumstances demand quick action. If we don't have time to assess a person's character, we need to get references from people he or she has worked with before. It is a mistake to not delegate, but probably an even more grievous mistake to delegate important tasks to the wrong people. Remember, you don't have to settle for second best. Wait for the best. Train for the best.

No one is perfect when we first put him or her to work. That's not what we're saying here. Those we delegate to, however, must possess the ability to learn and be teachable. They must also be willing. With these qualities, anything is possible. Even the most unlikely kinds of people are able to become enormously successful.

ANOINTING

We look for the anointing on a person in the area that we're considering them for. David, Moses, and Joshua were all anointed to lead the nation. The prophets throughout the Scripture were anointed to bring forth the Word of the Lord and to display signs and wonders that confirmed the Word. The priests were anointed to bring offerings and sacrifices to the Lord and make atonement for the people. It is possible that these people were not anointed for other duties.

When Uzziah stepped out of his anointing as king, attempting to carry out priestly functions, he was smitten with leprosy—judged by God. We are called to specific tasks and not others.

As leaders, we recognize what our people are anointed for. Some are anointed to lead prayer. When they pray, everyone else is stirred and prays along. Others, however, kill the prayer meeting. Everyone stops praying and listens to them instead of joining in the prayers. Some are anointed to lead worship, others are not; some are anointed for counseling, healing, organizing, leading, helping, and so on. We recognize, appoint, organize, develop, and deploy people into the specific tasks that they are anointed for.

The anointing enables people to actually do the job they're called to do. This anointing rests on people's lives so that they find themselves achieving far beyond their natural abilities. Sometimes those with experience hinder this supernatural element of power in their lives because they are not relying on God, but rather on their own talents. As we acknowledge our inadequacy for the job, we put ourselves in the place where we can be empowered by the Lord.

FRUITFULNESS

Some have thought that failure in business is confirmation they should be in the ministry. This is foolishness. If people have been successful in business, this will help them in ministry. If they have failed, then they need to overcome their defeat and learn success.

Proven people have submissive, teachable, cooperative, non-critical attitudes.

Charles Spurgeon refused applicants for ministry training who had failed in business. Position and title do not cause a person to be successful. A person may have the title of pastor or evangelist, but if the flock doesn't grow or people don't get saved, it reveals that they are missing it in their calling somewhere.

PRAYERFULNESS

We pray over our choices and sense that God is guiding our selection. Jesus spent the entire night in prayer before He chose His disciples, empowered them, defined their job description, and deployed them (Luke 6:12–13). The early church spent much time in prayer before sending out missionaries (Acts 13:3). Prayer helps us choose correctly.

Prayer brings the anointing that is essential for ministers to fulfill their calling. Prayer brings blessing upon our efforts for the Lord.

AFFINITY AND UNITY

The people we choose must display real unity with and affinity for the vision of the senior minister and the church. In the process of selecting people for roles in the church, we ask their opinion of the leadership, the rest of the team, and the church in general. We are not looking for yes-men, but if a person has problems with the senior minister and the church, then obviously he or she will cause problems on the team and in the church.

Many of the people around us will be from different backgrounds and cultures. This is not a problem, though. It is an affinity of spirit that we need, not sameness of style. If Christ is at the center of our fellowship, we are bonded together. Whoever buys into the vision God has for the congregation develops an affinity for all that is going on.

REASONS PEOPLE SHOULD NOT BE SELECTED

Being given positions on the team will not help "problem people." To think that appointments will heal bad attitudes is folly—they only reinforce the problems. Once a person holds a position, it is almost impossible to adjust his or her attitude.

This point is incredibly important. Too many times, pastors are emotionally coerced by someone's attitude into using that person against their better judgment. I'm aware of three distinct times when I've done this. The lesson takes time to learn. You see, I believe in people; I am always convinced that I can fix them. However, we've got to get people well before we give them the job, rather than attempting to heal them after they're in position.

If people are giving off the impression that they will cause trouble or leave the church if you don't give them a job, they will only cause deeper trouble for you once they have the job. This emotional blackmail will only continue and will escalate to all kinds of other matters. People find it harder to change once they hold positions than when they do not have responsibilities.

Don't give people tasks to keep them in the church. They should have prior commitments to the house of God that exceed titles and responsibilities.

Job Descriptions

Once jobs are delegated, the people should be told what their titles are (if any), what their responsibilities are, and to whom they are accountable. Further, the job description should identify their subordinates and what is required of them as well. This should be written out.

Once tasks are delegated, people need to receive clear instructions and training on what to do and how to do it. Once they begin carrying out their jobs, we need to keep in regular contact with them to assist them, not just to investigate. We need to be available to them at all times, helping them accomplish their jobs successfully.

These men and women should submit regular reports, perhaps on a weekly or monthly basis, outlining their progress and problems. We then go over these reports with them on a regular basis.

Building the Team

A great leader never polarizes the team on the basis of ethnicity, education, culture, or personality. A good leader actually places high value on the variety and the diversity of people on the team, realizing the vast benefits that are woven into this patchwork of personalities. The potential for a far wider sphere of influence increases with an expanding diversity of team members.

The difference between a boss and a leader is that a boss says, "Go!" and a leader, says "Let's go!" [103]

Here are some practical ways this principle is manifested:

1. THE LEADER BRINGS THE TEAM TOGETHER REGULARLY FOR INPUT.

Full-time staff members need to meet together at least once weekly. Great leaders don't live isolated from the team. Team members will only give grudging service if they feel cut off from their leader.

It is an affinity of spirit that we need, not sameness of style.

Teams thrive on attention from the top. Leaders are feeders.

Team building is not just about training and instruction, but also about giving hope, encouragement, recognition, and appreciation. Giving the members these four elements of reinforcement feeds the soul of the team. Team building comes from giving regular, positive attention to the team.

People easily drift from the true north of any organization. The leader needs to keep emphasizing the dream and the faith that "we can do it," as well as the strategies to achieve the goal, so that every member of the team is on board and feels that the entire team is in it together.

2. The leader must constantly reinforce and restate the vision.

Though the team may have heard it many times before, restating the vision keeps everyone focused on the right things. Whatever the leader speaks on, the vision is woven into the topic so that every subject is viewed with the philosophy and priorities of the ministry in mind.

3. Each individual receives recognition and public honor.

Recognition is absolutely essential with volunteer staff. One of the key skills leaders must have is not only the ability to get people to like them, but also the ability to get people to work with them. Great leaders inspire people to go the second and the third mile, to achieve goals, and to enjoy the experience.

In research carried out for their book *In Search of Excellence*, Peters and Waterman cite the finding that only 15 percent of workers are looking for higher wages. At the top of the list of what employees want is more recognition; a "better boss" comes next. [104]

Leaders foster respect and loyalty by simply recognizing and applauding the achievements of the individuals on the team. This can be as simple as announcing an accomplishment to everyone at a meeting. When hard work is rewarded, others on the team feel good about it also. One of their workmates has been recognized. The compact among coworkers is strengthened. People enjoy applauding one another.

4. The leader must be able to teach in the following areas:

❖ Kingdom Principles

❖ People Skills

❖ Success

❖ Relationships

❖ Expectations

A good leader should warn of things that can damage a good team. Clear direction comes regularly from the top.

5. THE LEADER INVOLVES THE TEAM MEMBERS IN DISCUSSIONS ABOUT EVENTS THAT AFFECT THEM ALL.

When every team member contributes to the final plan with ideas and strategies, they buy into the project. Once their input is respected, their energy and talents flow easily into the plan. The weight of the project is removed from the leader's shoulders and shared by the team.

Restating the vision keeps everyone focused on the right things.

Many leaders do not enjoy giving their dreams into the hands of others, but big dreams are never achieved without others. This is why many great aspirations die in the dust.

I often will have an idea I feel inspired about, and when I share it with the team, they knock it into a workable shape. I enjoy this experience because they all get to buy into what we're doing, rather than just being told what to do. Even if my idea doesn't look like I originally wanted it to, if I'm still getting the basic end result, then I'm happy. I can sacrifice a few sacred cows of my own and make a few compromises to the idea so that the team feels it is an integral part of what we're doing.

6. The leader trusts the team.

Problems affecting the congregation should be communicated to the team before they are made known to the rest of the church. Problems that don't affect the entire church can be made known to the team. Team members must realize that they are trusted. Then, they will rise to the occasion.

When every team member contributes to the project, they buy into it.

7. The leader heals relationships.

Any breaches between team members must be healed quickly before they infect others. A healed relationship is always stronger than it was before it fractured. We must get the concerned individuals together and reconcile them.

8. The leader admits his mistakes.

Confessions of failings and admissions of mistakes, when handled in the right way, win respect from our team members. If they feel we are being vulnerable with them in revealing our shortcomings, they will trust and support us.

9. The leader has personal integrity.

Personal integrity is what the team builds on more than anything else. Success is imperative for the morale of the team. Achieving goals is also imperative; but if integrity is compromised in the process, then team players will lose respect. When team members admire their leader, they are more than happy to give allegiance to that person.

10. THE LEADER DISCIPLINES IN LOVE.

Rebukes are carefully made and only reserved for anyone seriously stepping out of line. If a person's failure affects the rest of the group, everyone needs to be involved. If not, then the rebuke should be contained within the circle of offense. News of disciplinary action travels rapidly among a team.

Everyone must know there are boundaries and, if they are crossed, there are consequences. The credibility of a leader rests as much on the fact that he or she can encourage and build on truth as it does on his or her ability to rebuke, warn, correct, and recognize falsehood. The power of positive encouragement rests on the fact that we are also capable of discouraging or disciplining a person as well.

seventeen

THE LEADER IS A
DECISION MAKER

The price of greatness is responsibility.
—Sir Winston Churchill

I f we are leading, then we are making decisions. We accept responsibility for our own actions and for the people we lead. The key to making great decisions is to first accept the responsibility for solving the problem or achieving the dream. Great leaders don't blame others; they train others. Leaders are often blamed for the results, but then that's part of the job.

Sir Winston Churchill learned early to accept responsibility that wasn't even fairly dealt to him. When he was defeated in his first attempt at political office, winning the difficult seat of Oldham in Manchester, the party blamed its new candidate for the failure. His response was, "Everyone threw the blame on me. I have noticed they nearly always do. I suppose it is because they think I can bear it the best." [105] He also went on to say, "The price of greatness is responsibility." [106]

Someone has to make the decisions. That person is the leader. It's not just about making decisions; it's also about being decisive. Napoleon Bonaparte, Emperor of France in the nineteenth century and one of the greatest military commanders of all time, who conquered the larger part of Europe, said, "Hesitation and half-measures lose all in war." [107]

People who second-guess themselves, who hesitate, or who indulge in "buyer's remorse" forfeit the role of leading others because they have become unstable. James, the brother of Jesus Christ and leader of the great Jerusalem church, wrote,

> *But let him ask in faith, with no doubting, for he who doubts is like a wave of the sea driven and tossed by the wind. For let not that man suppose that he will receive anything from the Lord; he is a double-minded man, unstable in all his ways.* (James 1:6–8)

THE DEFINING DIFFERENCE BETWEEN LEADERS AND FOLLOWERS

Decision-making ability is possibly one of the few key ingredients that separate leaders from followers.

I've always admired Ronald Reagan as one of the great decisive leaders of our time. Prior to his assuming the office of President of the United States, his predecessors had hosted all kinds of talks with the Soviets, attempting to halt their expansionist policies. The Soviet Union would simply invade a country, hoist their flag, and take over. None of the "talks" achieved anything, however. Détente, SALT I, SALT II, the Camp David

Accords, and various summit meetings achieved little to nothing in preventing the USSR's progress and arms build-up.

When Reagan took office, he warned Colonel Muammar al-Qaddafi, the devout Muslim and anti-American Libyan military leader, that if he flew his planes out of restricted air space, U.S. fighters would shoot the Libyan planes down. The dictator didn't believe an American President would actually do anything differently than his predecessors had done. When Qaddafi's Air Force breached the restricted air space, Reagan ordered the planes shot out of the sky not once, but twice. The world sat up and paid attention. This man meant what he said and said what he meant. They thought, "He's decisive! He doesn't talk endlessly—he acts!"

Great leaders don't blame others; they train others.

The next crisis Reagan encountered was in his own country. The air traffic controllers throughout the U.S. threatened a strike. Reagan told them that if they went on strike, they would be in violation of federal laws, and he would therefore fire them all and bring in the military. The controllers didn't believe that this would happen, claiming that the military couldn't do the job. They said there would be aircraft accidents everywhere. They went on strike, Reagan fired them all, the military took over, and there was not one casualty in the sky.

No matter what other labels might be applied to him, President Reagan has to be called decisive. The ramifications of his decisive actions were enormous. He didn't want to talk incessantly with the Russians. The man did things! Before long, Russian military forces were vacating Afghanistan. The Russian red flag, which had gone up over eleven new countries under Nixon, began coming down in several oppressed nations. Communism itself began to crumble. The Berlin Wall finally toppled down. Obviously, there were other factors and other people involved in these events. There is no doubt, though, that decisive leadership brings about distinct change.

Once decisions are made, they should not be changed.

A good friend of mine, Peter Daniels, says to himself every morning as he rides the elevator, "Do it now!" My personal opinion is that decisions should not be made in a hurry. However, once they are made, they should not be changed. Leaders cannot afford to look like they're changing their minds or second-guessing themselves. Hold to the course.

I also know that all kinds of evil lurk in a vacuum. Any decision is better than no decision. A decision gets things moving. Once we're moving, God can guide us. He doesn't guide stationary Christians in the same way that we don't steer parked cars. There's a time to pray, and then there's a time to stop praying and start acting. At various times God told His servants to get up off their faces and act (Joshua 7:10).

A decision galvanizes a team. Not everyone on the team may like the decision, but at least the team has something to work toward. Because there is direction, forward movement is possible. Things get sorted out as the team members travel the path together. The person out front is the one who takes the responsibility and makes the decision. That person is you, the leader.

eighteen

THE ULTIMATE LEADER

I n writing to the Corinthian church, the apostle Paul outlined an important leadership principle when he instructed the saints at Corinth to *"follow my example, as I follow the example of Christ"* (1 Corinthians 11:1 NIV). Paul also extended the invitation to the Philippians to *"join in following my example, and note those who so walk, as you have us for a pattern"* (Philippians 3:17). Paul instructed the young pastor-leader Timothy to set a godly example for believers to follow as well:

> *Let no one despise your youth, but be an example to the believers in word, in conduct, in love, in spirit, in faith, in purity.* (1 Timothy 4:12)

From these and other verses, we see that it is essential for leaders to model godly behavior for others. And as disciples of Christ, we need to follow leaders who are following after Christ. Note that Paul cautioned the Corinthian believers to *"imitate"* (1 Corinthians 11:1 NKJV) or copy his behavior only as long as he was imitating Christ, who is our ultimate example and leader.

THE ULTIMATE EXAMPLE

Jesus is the ultimate example of how we are to live. He said, *"For I have given you an example, that you should do as I have done to you"* (John 13:15).

The apostle Peter echoed Paul's words about examples to follow when he wrote that we are called to follow in Christ's footsteps:

> *For you have been called for this purpose, since Christ also suffered for you, leaving you an example for you to follow in His steps.* (1 Peter 2:21 NASB)

**It is essential for leaders to model
godly behavior for others.**

In the end, Jesus is our ultimate example of leadership. We are to walk as He walked and act as He acted, mirroring His style.

THE ULTIMATE LEADERSHIP STYLE

Servant leadership, as exemplified by Jesus, is what every Christian leader is called to. This ultimate leadership style is one of humility and self-sacrifice. Paul discussed this when he wrote about the mind-set and heart attitudes we, as leaders, need to develop:

> *Let this mind be in you which was also in Christ Jesus, who, being in the form of God, did not consider it robbery*

*to be equal with God, but made Himself of no reputa-
tion, taking the form of a bondservant, and coming in
the likeness of men. And being found in appearance as
a man, He humbled Himself and became obedient to the
point of death, even the death of the cross.*

(Philippians 2:5–8)

Just as Christ humbled Himself by taking on the form of a
man—a bondservant, or a slave, no less—and gave up His life
for the human race, we likewise are to humble ourselves, set
aside our desires, and pour out our lives in service to others and
for the sake of God's kingdom.

*But he who is greatest among you shall be your servant.
And whoever exalts himself will be humbled, and he
who humbles himself will be exalted.*

(Matthew 23:11–12)

To become a great leader, each of us must first become
humble enough to serve others without any thought of self.

THE ULTIMATE LEADER

Jesus, our ultimate Leader, is leading us is to the cross,
where we are to die to self. Just as the apostle Paul declared,
"I die daily" (1 Corinthians 15:31), we are to do the same. We
are to respond with submissive spirits and absolute obedience
to the call of Christ:

*If anyone desires to come after Me, let him deny himself,
and take up his cross **daily**, and follow Me.*

(Luke 9:23, emphasis added)

Great leaders follow great leaders. As leaders and poten-
tially great leaders, we are to follow Christ by trading in our
desires, our dreams, our plans, and our titles for the cross He
gives us to carry and the destiny He has designed for us.

303

THE ULTIMATE CHOICE

If we are to become leaders in God's kingdom, Jesus calls us to make the ultimate choice, the ultimate sacrifice, for His sake and for the sake of the Gospel:

For whoever desires to save his life will lose it, but whoever loses his life for My sake and the gospel's will save it. (Mark 8:35)

Are you ready to die for the cause?

THE ULTIMATE VISION

I will build My church.
—Jesus of Nazareth

Jesus has a vision. He has a job to be done. He has determined to build His church. He calls men and women to work with Him to accomplish this dream. In the army of people He has enlisted are a breed called leaders.

To become a great leader, each of us must first become humble enough to serve others.

Jesus raises up people as servants to Himself and as leaders of His people in order to fulfill His dream. He raises this army to lead His flock. He raises leaders to carry the plan of salvation to the world. He raises leaders to organize His people and His work in this world.

God has lofty reasons for raising leaders. Jesus has declared that He will build His church: *"On this rock I will build My church, and the gates of Hades shall not prevail against it"* (Matthew 16:18). The rock of manifest revelation is what Jesus builds His church upon.

Manifest revelation is the flash of light from heaven that pierces the souls of men and women. This is light, the life of God Himself. It is like a piece of God to us. It is food for our spirits. It is what faith is because it is clear knowing—not just thinking or hoping. It is a deep inner knowledge from heaven above.

God's great leaders lead by revelation. Leaders must receive revelation from the Lord and take their people in that direction. It is vital that we understand what we are to preach, what we are to do, and what kind of organization we are to build through revelation from the Lord.

We must be motivated by the spiritual passion Jesus places within us. We need to build on the revelation God has given us, on our strengths, on who we are in Christ.

Good ideas are not good enough. They need to be God ideas. Just because someone else's methods work does not mean they will work for us. God plants a unique set of gifts within each of us as leaders, enabling us to do a particular work for Him in a particular way. If we deny those gifts, opting for something else that appeals to us, we forsake the means by which God wants to give us success (1 Timothy 4:14).

God builds His kingdom with people—not programs or methods, but people—godly men and women. Christ builds on the revelation of His truth living inside His people.

God's principles remain unchanged. He builds His great church upon living people. Jesus is building His church upon the living apostles, prophets, pastors, teachers, evangelists, and people of God. These are the men and women whose spiritual influence and gifts are pulsing through the body of Christ today.

Good ideas are not good enough. They need to be God ideas.

Leadership is the great, mysterious, wonderful gift that God is delivering to the army of men and women who are rising to lead our world to a brighter future in Him. As we pray and yield everything to the God of heaven, He equips us for this great calling on our lives.

> Give me a man of God—one man,
> Whose faith is master of his mind,
> And I will right all wrongs
> And bless the name of all mankind.
>
> Give me a man of God—one man,
> Whose tongue is touched with heaven's fire,
> And I will flame the darkest hearts
> With high resolve and clean desire.
>
> Give me a man of God—one man,
> One mighty prophet of the Lord,
> And I will give you peace on earth,
> Bought with a prayer and not a sword.
>
> Give me a man of God—one man,
> True to the vision that he sees,
> And I will build your broken shrines
> And bring the nations to their knees. [108]
>
> —George Liddell

ENDNOTES

[1] Oleh Butchatsky and James C. Sarros, *Leadership: Australia's CEOs: Finding Out What Makes Them the Best* (Sydney: HarperBusiness, 1996), 130.

[2] Philip Selznick, *Leadership and Administration* (New York: Harper & Row, 1985), 1957.

[3] David McClelland, *Power, the Inner Experience* (New York: John Wiley & Sons, 1976), 84–85.

[4] Thomas Peters and Robert Waterman Jr., *In Search of Excellence* (New York: Harper & Row, 1985), 26.

[5] Charles G. Finney, *Lectures on Revival* (Bloomington, Minn.: Bethany House, 1988), 48.

[6] <http://www.elizabethi.org/uk/armada/>

[7] E. M. Bounds, *Power through Prayer* (New Kensington, Pa.: Whitaker House, 1982), 31.

[8] Eddie Gibbs, *I Believe in Church Growth* (London: Hodder & Stoughton, 1981), 130.

[9] E. M. Bounds, *Power through Prayer* (New Kensington, Pa.: Whitaker House, 1982), 8.

[10] John Edmund Haggai, *Lead On! Leadership That Endures in a Changing World* (Dallas: Word Books, 1986), 6.

[11] Thomas Peters and Robert Waterman Jr., *In Search of Excellence* (New York: Harper & Row, 1985), 85.

[12] C. Peter Wagner, *Church Growth: State of the Art* (Wheaton, Ill.: Tyndale House, 1986), 197.

[13] George Barna, *Church Marketing* (Ventura, Ca.: Regal Books, 1992), 119.

[14] Compiled from Strong's #G3539 and *Young's Analytical Concordance.*

[15] Paul Yonggi Cho, *The Fourth Dimension* (Plainfield, N.J.: Logos International, 1979), 24.

16 C. Peter Wagner, "Why Body Evangelism Really Works," *Global Church Growth Bulletin*, May/June 1983, 271.

17 Paul Yonggi Cho, *The Fourth Dimension* (Plainfield, N.J.: Logos International, 1979).

18 James Montgomery, *DAWN 2000: Seven Million Churches to Go* (Pasadena, Ca.: William Carey Library Publishers, 1989), 144–145. A downloadable PDF document of this out-of-print book can be found on the Internet at <http://www.dawnministries.org/documents/files/books/13%20Steps.PDF>

19 C. Peter Wagner, *Church Growth: State of the Art* (Wheaton, Ill.: Tyndale House, 1986), 202.

20 "Jack William Nicklaus," *Microsoft® Encarta*, © 1994 Microsoft Corporation. © 1994 Funk & Wagnall's Corporation.

21 William Barclay, *The Gospel of Matthew,* vol. 1, *The Daily Study Bible Series,* rev. ed. (Philadelphia: Westminster Press, 1975), 225.

22 *Jamieson, Fausset and Brown's Commentary* (Grand Rapids, Mich.: Zondervan, 1961), 891.

23 Flavius Josephus, "Antiquities of the Jews," 15.11.5, *Josephus: The Complete Works* (Nashville: Nelson, 1998), 509.

24 Charles G. Finney, *Lectures on Revival* (Bloomington, Minn.: Bethany House, 1988), 79.

25 Charles H. Spurgeon, *Lectures to My Students on the Art of Preaching* (London: Marshall, Morgan & Scott, 1989).

26 Stanley Howard Frodsham, *Smith Wigglesworth, Apostle of Faith* (Springfield, Mo.: Gospel Publishing House, 1990), 135.

27 William Shakespeare, *As You Like It*, Act II, Scene VII.

28 Abraham Lincoln, as quoted by Donald T. Phillips, *Lincoln on Leadership: Executive Strategies for Tough Times* (New York: Warner Books, 1992).

29 "Fun Keeps You Fit," *The Daily Telegraph* (Sydney, Australia), Monday, February 24, 1997.

30 Francis of Assisi, *A Day in Your Presence, Devotional Readings Arranged by David Hazard,* (Bloomington, Minn.: Bethany House Publishers, 1992).

31 C. S. Lewis, *The Screwtape Letters* (New York: Collier Books, 1982).

[32] Janet Lowe, *Jack Welch Speaks: Wisdom from the World's Greatest Business Leader* (Hoboken, N.J.: John Wiley & Sons, 1998), 170.

[33] <http://www.dcmilitary.com/navy/journal/7_25/commentary/17692-1.html>

[34] Noah Webster, *On the Education of Youth in America*, 1788. <http://www.presidentialprayerteam.-org/index.php>

[35] Geoffrey Kells, as quoted in Oleh Butchatsky and James C. Sarros, *Leadership: Australia's CEOs: Finding Out What Makes Them the Best* (Sydney: HarperBusiness 1996), 222.

[36] <http://www.plumbingstore.com/quotes.html>

[37] <http://www.plumbingstore.com/quotes-harrytruman.html>

[38] Janet Lowe, *Jack Welch Speaks: Wisdom from the World's Greatest Business Leader* (Hoboken, N.J.: John Wiley & Sons, 1998), 152.

[39] Philip Baker, *Secrets of Super Achievers* (New Kensington, Pa.: Whitaker House, 2005), 132

[40] John Maxwell, *Developing the Leader within You* (Nashville: Nelson, 1993), 35.

[41] Oleh Butchatsky and James C. Sarros, *Leadership: Australia's CEOs: Finding Out What Makes Them the Best* (Sydney: HarperBusiness 1996), 15.

[42] John Maxwell, *Developing the Leader within You* (Nashville: Nelson, 1993), 36, 37.

[43] <http://www.milmin.com/resources/leadership/LeadershipStudies/1-Integrity.htm>

[44] John Maxwell, *Developing the Leader within You* (Nashville: Nelson, 1993), 40.

[45] <http://www.beargrass.org/sermons/s033003.html>

[46] Oleh Butchatsky and James C. Sarros, *Leadership: Australia's CEOs: Finding Out What Makes Them the Best* (Sydney: HarperBusiness 1996), 246.

[47] <http://www.chriscarey.com/noundo.html>

[48] <http://www.brainyquote.com/quotes/quotes/b/billygraha161989.html>

[49] <http://www.motivatingquotes.com/character.htm>

[50] <http://www.famous-motivational-quotes.com/sports-motivational-quotes.html>

[51] <http://www.leadershipdigest.com/quotes/quotes.htm>

[52] Charles H. Spurgeon, *Lectures to My Students on the Art of Preaching* (London: Marshall, Morgan & Scott, 1989), 214, 225.

[53] <http://quotations.about.com/od/stillmorefamouspeople/a/JohnDRockefell1.htm>

[54] Philip Baker, *Secrets of Super Achievers* (New Kensington, Pa.: Whitaker House, 2005), 133.

[55] Chuck Colson, *Parliamentary Prayer Breakfast*, Canberra, Australia, 17 November 1997.

[56] Keith A. Craver, et. al., "Ten Propositions Regarding Leadership" (Air Command and Staff College Directorate of Research, 1996), 21. <http://www.au.af.mil/au/awc/awcgate/acsc/96-079.pdf.>

[57] <http://www.selfhelpmagazine.com/articles/stress/meditate/adverse4.html>

[58] Stephen Mansfield, *Never Give In: The Extraordinary Character of Winston Churchill* (Elkton, MD: Highland Books, 1995), 183–184.

[59] James C. Hume, *The Wit and Wisdom of Winston Churchill* (New York: HarperCollins Publishers, 1994), 23.

[60] Bob Rotella with Bob Cullen, *Golf Is Not a Game of Perfect* (New York: Simon & Schuster, 1995).

[61] Andy Stanley, *The Next Generation Leader* (Sisters, Or.: Multnomah Publishers Inc., 2003), 51, 52.

[62] Dan Millman, "On Courage," in *Chicken Soup for the Soul*, eds. Jack Canfield and Mark Victor Hansen (Deerfield Beach, Fla.: Health Communications, Inc., 1993).

[63] <http://www.thinkarete.com/quotes/by_category/love/leadership/>

[64] Edwin Lewis Cole, "Strong Men in Tough Times," *Charisma*, July 1993, 28. Adapted from *Strong Men in Tough Times* (Lake Mary, Fla.: Creation House, 1993).

[65] Helen Wessel, *Charles Finney* (Bloomington, Minn.: Bethany House, 1997), 184.

[66] *People's Needs, Hopes, and Fears: A Survey of Public Attitudes, Sydney and Melbourne,* January 1992. Prepared by Quadrant Research Services for the Sydney City Mission, January 1992.

[67] David Gelman, "Counting Your Blessings: Psychologists take up the pursuit of happiness," *Newsweek*, 24 May 1993, vol. 121 Issue 21, 76.

[68] Hugh Mackay, *Reinventing Australia: After the Federal Election Seminar*, The Sydney Institute, Tuesday, May 4, 1993.

[69] Steven Covey, *The Seven Habits of Highly Effective People* (New York: Simon & Schuster, 1989).

[70] "Ralph Waldo Emerson," *Microsoft® Encarta*, © 1994 Microsoft Corporation. © 1994 Funk & Wagnall's Corporation.

[71] Charles W. Eliot, as quoted by Dale Carnegie, *How to Win Friends and Influence People* (New York: Simon and Schuster, 1981), 77. <http://www.targetitmarketing.com/ebooks/pdfs/how-to-win-friends.pdf>

[72] Dale Carnegie, *How to Win Friends and Influence People* (New York: Simon and Schuster, 1981), 80. <http://www.targetitmarketing.com/ebooks/pdfs/how-to-win-friends.pdf>

[73] Gerald S. Nirenberg, *Getting Through to People* (Englewood Cliffs, N.J.: Prentice-Hall, 1963), 31.

[74] Donald Phillips, *Lincoln on Leadership: Executive Strategies for Tough Times* (New York: Warner Books, 1992), 31.

[75] Charles H. Spurgeon, *Lectures to My Students on the Art of Preaching* (London: Marshall, Morgan & Scott, 1989), 329.

[76] Donald Phillips, *Lincoln on Leadership: Executive Strategies for Tough Times* (New York: Warner Books, 1992).

[77] <http://www.friendship.com.au/quotes/quohis.html>

[78] Dale Carnegie, *How to Win Friends and Influence People* (New York: Simon and Schuster, 1981), 65. <http://www.targetitmarketing.com/ebooks/pdfs/how-to-win-friends.pdf>

[79] <http://www.mitchellmeredith.co.uk/aboutus/phil.htm>

[80] <http://www.lovethissite.com/asmile/>

[81] Janet Lowe, *Jack Welch Speaks: Wisdom from the World's Greatest Business Leader* (Hoboken, N.J.: John Wiley & Sons, 1998), 159.

[82] Richard Wurmbrand, *Sermons in Solitary Confinement* (London: Hodder & Stoughton, 1969).

[83] Oleh Butchatsky and James C. Sarros, *Leadership: Australia's CEOs: Finding Out What Makes Them the Best* (Sydney: HarperBusiness 1996), 131.

[84] Marshall McLuhan, *Understanding Media: The Extensions of Man* (New York: McGraw-Hill, 1964).

[85] < http://www.bestinspirationalquotes.com/success-leaders/winston-churchill.htm>

[86] Winston Churchill, as quoted by Stephen Mansfield, *Never Give In: The Extraordinary Character of Winston Churchill* (Elkton, Md.: Highland Books, 1995), 138.

[87] <http://www.small-business-options.com/business.html>

[88] Oleh Butchatsky and James C. Sarros, *Leadership: Australia's CEOs: Finding Out What Makes Them the Best* (Sydney: HarperBusiness 1996), 248.

[89] Trump, Donald, *Trump: The Art of the Deal* (New York: Random House).

[90] <http://www.quotedb.com/quotes/2419>

[91] William Shakespeare, *King Richard II*, Act V, Scene V.

[92] <http://www.bplans.com/targetonline/index.cfm?s=specs&id=7&affiliate=sba>

[93] *Success* – March, 1988.

[94] Dr. Richard A. Swenson, *Margin: Restoring Emotional, Physical, Financial and Time Reserves to Overloaded Lives* (Colorado Springs: NavPress, 1995).

[95] Steve Farrar, *Finishing Strong* (Sisters, Ore.: Multnomah Books, 1995), 150.

[96] "Oscar Wilde," "The Ballad of Reading Gaol," *Microsoft® Encarta,* © 1994, Microsoft Corporation, © 1994, Funk & Wagnall's Corporation.

[97] John Maxwell, *Injoy Club Audio Tape.*

[98] <http://www.ndrs.org/physicsonline/humour/bricks.htm>

[99] Paul Kregel, *Maier Josephus, The Essential Works*, (Grand Rapids, Mich.: Kregel, 1994), 48, 49.

[100] <http://www.fbcshelbyville.com/templates/gen03re/details.asp?id=27888&PID=162649>

[101] David Paul Yonggi Cho, *Successful Home Cell Groups* (Bridge Publishing, 1981), 11.

[102] William Bradford, Plymouth Plantation, 1620-1647 (New York: Modern Library, McGraw-Hill, 1981).

[103] Oleh Butchatsky and James C. Sarros, *Leadership: Australia's CEOs: Finding Out What Makes Them the Best* (Sydney: HarperBusiness 1996), 4.

[104] Thomas Peters and Robert Waterman Jr., *In Search of Excellence* (New York: Harper & Row, 1985).

[105] Stephen Mansfield, *Never Give In: The Extraordinary Character of Winston Churchill* (Elkton, Md.: Highland Books, 1995), 52.

[106] <http://www.quotationspage.com/quotes/Sir_Winston_Churchill/>

[107] <http://www.napoleon-series.org/research/napoleon/c_quotes.html>

[108] < http://www.s-g-m.net/leaders1.htm>

About the Author

PHIL PRINGLE

Phil Pringle is the Senior Minister of Christian City Church Oxford Falls in Sydney, Australia, and the founder and president of Christian Church International (C3i). Originally from New Zealand, Phil and his wife, Christine, started Christian City Church (CCC) in 1980.

From small beginnings, CCC has grown to become one of the largest and most influential churches in Australia. Globally, the CCC movement now consists of over 100 churches spread throughout Australia and New Zealand, North America, Asia, and Europe. The entire movement of vibrant churches has been birthed as a result of Phil's leadership and vision.

Phil's dynamic and relevant preaching has made him a much sought after speaker in both Christian and secular contexts. He is particularly noted for his insights on topics such as faith, leadership, the ministry of the Holy Spirit, church building, and kingdom principles of finance and giving. Phil and his wife live in Sydney's north beaches region. They have three children.

The Principles and Power of Vision
Dr. Myles Munroe

Whether you are a businessperson, a homemaker, a student, or a head of state, best-selling author Dr. Myles Munroe explains how you can make your dreams and hopes a living reality. Your success is not dependent on the state of the economy or what the job market is like. You do not need to be hindered by the limited perceptions of others or by a lack of resources. Discover time-tested principles that will enable you to fulfill your vision no matter who you are or where you come from.

You were not meant for a mundane or mediocre life. Revive your passion for living, pursue your dream, discover your vision—and find your true life.

ISBN: 0-88368-951-0 • Hardcover • 240 pages

www.whitakerhouse.com

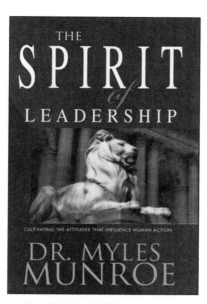

The Spirit of Leadership
Dr. Myles Munroe

Leaders may be found in boardrooms, but they may also be found in families, schools, and organizations of all kinds—anywhere people interact, nurture, create, or build. Contrary to popular opinion, leadership is not meant for an elite group of people who—by fate or accident—are allowed to be leaders while everyone else is consigned to being lifelong followers. After personally training thousands of leaders from around the world, best-selling author Dr. Myles Munroe reports that while all people possess leadership potential, many do not understand how to cultivate the leadership nature and how to apply it to their lives. Discover the unique attitudes that all effective leaders exhibit, how to eliminate hindrances to your leadership abilities, and how to fulfill your particular calling in life. With wisdom and power, Dr. Munroe reveals a wealth of practical insights that will move you from being a follower to becoming the leader you were meant to be!

ISBN: 0-88368-983-9 • Hardcover • 304 pages

www.whitakerhouse.com

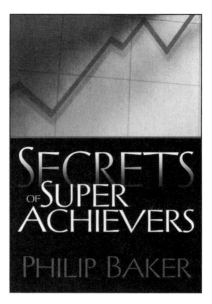

Secrets of Super Achievers
Philip Baker

Have you ever noticed someone who seems to have it all—a great family, financial security, and an adventurous outlook on new challenges? A great life does not happen by accident—it is chosen and requires desire, determination, and faith. Those who refuse to let life happen to them, but instead choose to make life happen, boldly break away from the security of mediocrity and eagerly chase God's best for their lives. Philip Baker provides insight and direction for those seeking to be more than just average and greater than the status quo. He shows readers the secrets to perseverance, balance, focus, endurance, and courage, all with a humor and wisdom that compels and enlightens.

ISBN: 0-88368-806-9 • Hardcover • 192 pages

www.whitakerhouse.com

www.deepercalling.com

Power Points for Success
Bob Harrison

Let one of America's most effective motivational speakers help you improve or completely transform your life—one step at a time. In his signature enthusiastic style, Bob Harrison guides you through a variety of life's challenges, revealing how you can be an overcomer and experience increase in every area of your life. Bob's principles of increase show how to change your mind-set and build yourself up so that you can live a victorious life—physically, mentally, financially, spiritually, and relationally. Through his success strategies, Bob has positively impacted homes, businesses, and organizations around the nation and world. With *Power Points,* you can benefit from these same strategies. As you activate the truths in this book—presented in a practical and easy-to-understand manner—your life can take on dramatic new direction and power.

ISBN: 0-88368-406-3 • Hardcover • 240 pages

www.whitakerhouse.com

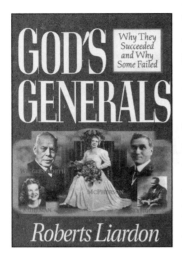

God's Generals:
Why They Succeeded and Why Some Failed
Roberts Liardon

Some of the most powerful ministers ever to ignite the fires of revival did so by dynamically demonstrating the Holy Spirit's power. Roberts Liardon faithfully chronicles the lives and spiritual journeys of twelve of *God's Generals,* including William J. Seymour, the son of ex-slaves, who turned a tiny horse stable on Azusa Street, Los Angeles, into an internationally famous center of revival; Aimee Semple McPherson, the glamorous, flamboyant founder of the Foursquare Church and the nation's first Christian radio station; and Smith Wigglesworth, the plumber who read no book but the Bible—and raised the dead!

ISBN: 0-88368-944-8 • Hardcover • 416 pages

God's Generals II:
The Roaring Reformers
Roberts Liardon

The basic truths of the Protestant faith—the things you believe and base your life on—were not always accepted and readily taught. Here are six of *God's Generals* who fought to reestablish the core beliefs and principles of the early church in an atmosphere of oppression, ignorance, and corruption that pervaded the medieval church. As you read about these *Roaring Reformers,* men who sacrificed everything in their fight for God, you will appreciate the freedom you have to worship, find encouragement for your spiritual battles, and be motivated to find biblical truth in your own life.

ISBN: 0-88368-945-6 • Hardcover • 416 pages